IMAGES OF ENGLAND

CREWE PUBS

IMAGES OF ENGLAND

CREWE PUBS

HOWARD CURRAN

TEMPUS

Frontispiece: Howard researching in the Crown Hotel in Earle Street.

Front cover: Raven Inn, Dewes Street, *c*.1897.

First published 2004

Tempus Publishing Limited
The Mill, Brimscombe Port,
Stroud, Gloucestershire, GL5 2QG
www.tempus-publishing.com

British Library Cataloguing in Publication Data.
A catalogue record for this book is available from the British Library.

ISBN 0 7524 3254 0

Typesetting and origination by Tempus Publishing Limited.
Printed in Great Britain.

Contents

Acknowledgements

Local historians and townspeople from the past have greatly influenced my thoughts on what the watering holes of Crewe meant to the town. Having read books, essays and writings from numerous early town inhabitants, I have been able to see how the pub has played its part in the progression of this town. Without these early writings and reminiscences my research would have probably been much harder, if not impossible. I am therefore eternally grateful to all the former residents/historians of the area whose writings I have been privileged to read.

I am particularly indebted to former residents: Richard Lindop, Martin Heath and Dr. Chaloner. Even an article written by *Antiquarian* at the beginning of the twentieth century was of guidance in colouring in the picture of life during that time. A number of years ago, looking almost with awe at the photographic evidence of Albert Hunn from the 1960s, encouraged a colleague and myself to try to acquire photographic evidence of our own. Therefore, I would like to record a special thanks to the scores of Crewe residents who have, over many years, been of help and assistance to me. My colleague and myself are especially grateful to those residents who have allowed us to copy their photographs, enabling us to build a collection which we believe is quite unique.

I have been tremendously assisted in my continuing quest for information by perusing the local papers and reference books. The archived local newspapers, *Crewe Chronicles* and the *Guardian* have been well preserved by the staff of Crewe library who therefore deserve a mention; but special thanks must be given to the former Chief Librarian, Geoff Pimlett, for all his help and assistance. The Almanacs of Wilmot Eardley, stored in the Library have also been a great source of information that shouldn't go unnoticed. Finally, my thanks go to all the publicans, past and present, for their help and memories.

All photographs in this book are taken from the collection of Howard Curran/ Michael Gilsenan and all copyright therefore remains with them.

Howard Curran, 2004

Introduction

Until the Grand Junction Railway Company decided to use Crewe as its halfway point between Earlstown and Birmingham, very little is officially known about the area. Whilst there was never an ancient town or village of Crewe, there were the hamlets of Monks and Church Coppenhall. Before the railways arrived, Crewe itself was little more than a small cluster of buildings consisting of a few farm labourers' dwellings and around a dozen farmhouses, dominated by the impressive Crewe Hall. On its border sat Monks Coppenhall whilst adjoining that boundary was Church Coppenhall. Both, as is now well-known, would eventually become Crewe although at different stages in their history.

Even the decision to use Crewe as the halfway point is seemingly shrouded in some mystery. Some leading railway officials felt that it would be easier to go through Nantwich and Market Drayton and on into Birmingham. However, even preliminary enquiries cause strong opposition from local canal and landowners alike. Although the opposition to their plans was disappointing, it became clear that because of the heavy clay of Monks Coppenhall area, that route would be more suitable for their heavy machinery. That decision certainly didn't suit Lord Crewe for he too didn't want the railways across his land, and it took an Act of Parliament to convince him otherwise.

Although actual firm dating of the town is extremely difficult, it is generally recognised that parts of Monks Coppenhall had become commonly known as Crewe soon after the railway station had been built. Nowadays for convenience, most modern historians use the date of the arrival of the first train in 1837 as the beginning of the town's history. Early maps show clearly that the first railway workers settled in and around the Christ Church area of Monks Coppenhall, eventually spreading in a mainly westerly direction. Understanding Crewe's beginnings becomes that much easier by looking at local street names. It then becomes noticeable that most streets in Monks Coppenhall invariably have names with a railway connection; Church Coppenhall, on the other hand, has names associated with the local clergy, farmers and landowners.

In the ten years from 1851 to 1861, a considerable number of houses and pubs were constructed outside of the Company's estate. This created urgent problems for those residents living outside the Company's domain. These problems included basic problems

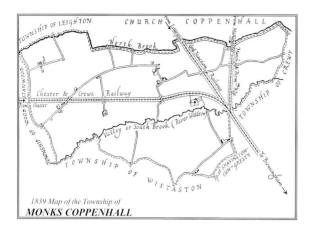

1839 Map of the Township of
MONKS COPPENHALL

Map of the township
of Monks Coppenhall,
1839.

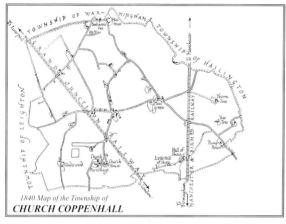

1840 Map of the Township of
CHURCH COPPENHALL

Map of the township
of Church Coppenhall,
1840.

with water supply, sewage disposal, lighting requirements and road/pavement maintenance. It was in the background of these problems that the township of Monks Coppenhall adopted the Local Government Act of 1858 to become self-governing; Church Coppenhall, however, refused to take part. In 1860, the first meeting of this Board took place in the Mechanics Institute and adopted the name of The Monks Coppenhall Local Board. Nine years later, in 1869, it changed its name to The Crewe Local Board.

After this event, some semblance of order appeared within local government. It nevertheless became apparent that to completely govern itself, Crewe needed to be incorporated into a Borough. That incorporation took place in 1877 but still using the old Monks Coppenhall boundary. My first thoughts were to base this book on Crewe's pubs, using that 1877 Monks Coppenhall (Crewe) boundary. However, as that may have eliminated quite a number of residents' favourites I decided to use the 1936 boundaries instead. It was nearly sixty years after the incorporation that the rest of Church Coppenhall and other surrounding areas became part of Crewe. Ironically, that was also the year that Crewe station at last became part of Crewe.

Local history reveals very little on Inns or Taverns in either of the Coppenhalls. Records do however indicate that a number of Inns existed before the arrival of the railways. Church Coppenhall had the Horse Shoe, the Cross Keys and the Blue Bell Inn and, up to the beginning of the nineteenth century, also the Black Horse Inn to add to the equation. The only other known pub in the vicinity was the George Hotel and on the Woolstanwood boundary. Those few Inns and Taverns would be more than enough to suit the alcoholic requirements of that period.

Just how well they did suit is shown in the 1831 census returns, which reveals that Monks Coppenhall had 148 residents whilst Church Coppenhall had 350. Ten years later, because of the impending arrival of railway workers, that figure had altered dramatically. Monks Coppenhall's population alone had increased to just over 1,000, whilst Church Coppenhall's residents now totalled some 500. Eight years later the population of Monks Coppenhall had become nearly 5,000 which created a need for more alcoholic, and consequently leisure, outlets.

Although it's difficult to discover any named Inns within the original Monks Coppenhall boundary, scant records of the time do indicate a number of unnamed beerhouses. It appears there were two on Nantwich Road, situated roughly where the British Lion and the Earl of Crewe are now. There was one in Mill Lane (Mill Street) near to the present Union Street, whilst a fourth was on Lower Nantwich Road (West Street), near to Merrill's Bridge.

The first pub built in the new town of Crewe was the Royal Hotel in 1840, with the Grand Junction, the Red Bull or the Adelphi being a close second, third and fourth. It is difficult to show in which order they were built because the original thirteen were constructed at quite a brisk pace. Census returns show quite clearly that by 1850 all thirteen were completed (refer to page 29 for the complete list). All these pubs being built at the same time was, of course, no coincidence. The first railway workers had been transferred from Edgehill in March 1843 and their needs had to be addressed. Their arrival, in addition to the hundreds of construction workers already residing here, some for over three years, created a large demand for pubs.

The few short years since the arrival of the railway's workforce had brought a population boom unequalled almost anywhere else in England. In these circumstances, it's not surprising to learn that the role of the public house in the town's social fabric became an important ingredient. It was felt by many at the time as an accepted way of escapism from the toils and drudgery of their daily work. The public house offered refreshment relaxation and entertainment but, more importantly, it offered them a social gathering point.

Nineteenth-century Crewe was no different from anywhere else in the country in the fact that any form of leisure activity outside the public house was very limited. The only other possible serious alternative was one of the various religious outlets and their activities. In simple terms, during this period most people's social relaxation relied on either the pub or the church. This led to feelings of uneasiness between the two, which many believed was never really addressed. Neither seemed prepared to tackle the animosity.

Throughout this period, people usually in authority were concerned about what they felt was the level of 'drunkenness'. They believed it was widespread amongst the working classes. However, many felt they had no real understanding of the problems of the day and the working man's need for relaxation in readiness for his following day's work. In Crewe, some railway officials saw a few drunkards as a major epidemic when, in reality, the vast majority of men visiting the pub were moderate and disciplined in their drinking habits. This was especially true in this town where, for the vast majority, attending work in a sober condition was of major importance.

Records show that even in the worst years, only just over 150 people per annum were prosecuted for drunkenness. Although these figures look quite high in isolation it must be remembered the population of the Borough at the time was nearly 40,000. In any case,

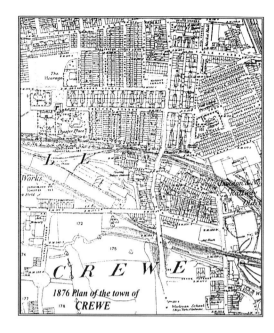

Map of the town of Crewe, 1876.

prosecutions for this offence in Crewe were lower that most other urbanised areas. Some misguided local people at the time believed that these low figures were due to the police being somewhat lenient; this could never be proven and maybe, as very often happens in these circumstances, some people just overreacted to the situation.

The town's population increases obviously took place in stages. The alcoholic and relaxation needs of different localities were addressed as and when needed. Eventually, the number of pubs within the town reached its saturation point of just over ninety. Over the years, that figure has fluctuated one way or another but usually, there has been between eighty-five and ninety in existence at any one time. The 1903 Licensing Session for the Borough was told that there were ninety-two pubs at that time for a population of 42,000. For obvious reasons, the number of pubs has reduced dramatically over the last forty years, and the town now has about fifty-six – even whilst this book is being compiled, some are in serious trouble and close to closure. The reasons for the decline is due to many factors, none more important than the many other alternative leisure pursuits that are now being provided.

This book will demonstrate how during the nineteenth and early twentieth century, the pub was probably the major player in the town's social activities. A town famous for its engineering skills needs its workforce to relax ready for the toils of the next day. The pub and its social activities provided what many of the ordinary workingmen needed, a place to relax and unwind. For all its bad publicity (and it has had its fair share) it was for many years, their only real leisure outlet.

This book was never intended to be about how pubs only served the people's alcoholic needs – that would be an injustice. Hopefully, it will explain how the pub was an integral part of the town's past. To fully understand that implication, pubs are included within the areas they served and the local people that used them. The book will record for future generations of our Borough that not only were many of them a major player in the town's social life; some were part of the town's architectural history.

one

Earlier Inns

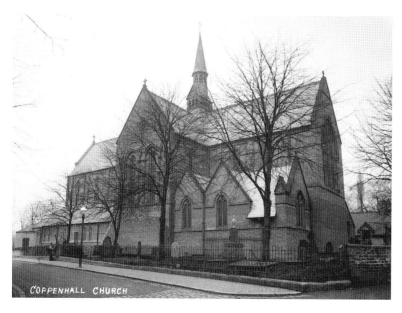

COPPENHALL CHURCH

St Michael's Church, Ford Lane.(Path leads to the former Blue Bell Inn), 1907.

Like many old buildings, St Michael's Church is surrounded in mystery and mystique. Even its foundation is clouded in some obscurity; a number of former historians have questioned the reliability of the first-known date of 1373. They quote various other dates ranging from 650 to 1111 as the possible foundation of the church. What is officially known is that a chapel-of-ease to St. Chad's Wybunbury was established in the late fourteenth century.

The first St Michael's Church was a timber-framed structure built using the method of wattle and daub in its construction. Records show it was possibly more westerly than the present church. It measured fifty feet by thirty feet, and was thirty feet high. On its eastern boundary were three farm labourers' cottages. They were quite basic in design and certainly not very picturesque, however; towards the end of the late sixteenth century, it seems that one labourer began to sell home-made beer. Out of this early venture, the area's old pub, the Blue Bell Inn, would eventually arise.

The original Blue Bell Inn situated in Sandy Lane (Broad Street) was surrounded in its own charisma. Many interesting facts appear from its colourful past perhaps none greater than what happened during the Civil War. On the 5 February 1644, Yeomen from Cross Green, Maw Green and homesteads around the Church joined forces with the Nantwich supporters of the Parliamentarians (Roundheads), on the corner of Mill Street (Mill Lane) and Nantwich Road. Under the leadership of Sir Ranulphe Crewe, they intended to march to Crewe Hall and successfully rout out the Royalist who had captured it a few weeks earlier. It is well-recorded that after the battle was won, the local yeoman heartily quaffed their ale to their success, in none other than the Blue Bell Inn.

The second Church of St Michael was built in 1821. Around this time, the Inn was substantially improved and a more substantial building was constructed. The new Blue Bell became the centre of attraction being used for all kinds of functions. A good example is the second Annual Celery Show, held there on 26 September 1874. The show, which was well-patronised by the locals, was followed by an excellent dinner provided by the landlord, Mr Latham. Afterwards, local artists gave their renditions of well-known songs, and everyone agreed they provided excellent entertainment. It was felt by everybody there that the whole event had been an astounding success and hopefully would carry on for many years to come.

In 1904, suddenly and to the dismay of the locals, its licence was withdrawn and this celebrated pub never opened its doors again. Although never used again as a pub, the building itself remained in existence for a further thirty years until in 1938, becaue of its dangerous condition of lying derelict for many years, it was eventually demolished.

No history of this area would be complete without reference to Bridget Bostock, the White Witch of Coppenhall. In 1748, Bridget was a nationwide figure for her reputed activities as a faith healer. It was alleged she was able to cure all kinds of illnesses and wounds by prayer and her saliva glands. The method she used of licking the wounds with her saliva was similar to the method used by most animals. She is reputed to have been born during the seventeenth century and died towards the middle of the next century. Almost everything about her is shrouded in mystery – no one has ever established her official birth or death. Past local historians have searched through the parish records but failed to reveal any records of her christening or burial, as though she never existed, although the national press of 1748 did carry articles about her exploits. At the height of her fame, it was reputed she had a doorkeeper admitting her clients five or six at a time. Patients would arrive from many towns and villages all over the country using the local Inns for their refreshments, the Blue Bell possibly being one of their favourite haunts.

The Black Horse Inn, built in 1769, was also in Sandy Lane and about a quarter of a mile from Cross Green. When originally built, it was both a farmhouse and inn. On visiting the property some twenty-odd years ago, its time as an Inn was still quite

The Black Horse Inn, Broad Street, c. 1957.

evident. A close inspection revealed that despite numerous alterations, its former tap room and beer cellar were still quite obvious. I found this quite surprising considering that on the death of the landlord in the early nineteenth century, it became just a farmhouse. It has seen many owners during its existence until it fell into the ownership of the Hancock family in 1935. After they vacated, only a few years ago, it was extensively renovated. It now bears no resemblance whatsoever to any of its former uses, but the memory lives on.

. . . .

Most residents who remember the Chetwode believed it was a seventeenth-century coaching Inn. That was not so because when the first railway workers arrived, it was a typical Cheshire farmhouse, fronting the road that led down to the west of the area. Many of these early railwaymen would use the farm to buy dairy and greengrocer products from the local farmer, Benjamin Mulliner.

Mulliner, who vacated the farm in early 1870, moved into 9 Albert Street where he remained until his death in 1884. However, before his death he would witness a great deal of development in the Hightown area, such as the farm's conversion into a pub with William Robinson as its first landlord. Reputedly built in 1620, there is no reason to doubt that it was a farm. After Mulliner's departure it ceased farming activities and was converted into the pub that is so well remembered. During its conversion into an Inn, the front was vastly extended with a large turret-bay front lounge bar being added.

Some years after its conversion, a local writer commented on the Inn, saying, 'it had been altered to suit the vandalistic tastes of the nineteenth-century licensed victualler, whose only interest was in creating facilities for quick and convenient dispensation of alcoholic refreshments'.

In the next paragraph, however, he appears to have justified the conversion by saying, 'in carrying out the improvements, the architect had preserved a great deal of the original building. He has managed to create an old-fashioned hostelry with an up-to-date finish. Half-timbered and plastered with cross-gable red-tiled roof and porch, it was indeed a very pleasant place to look upon. The improvements along with the open space created at the front protected by chains, complete with a sign, boldly proclaiming "The Chetwode Arms" leaves very little else to be desired'.

He finished the article by saying, 'the enterprising architect had surpassed himself with the figured representation on the foot of the chimney by the doorway. Of anyone entering into the enclosure, his or her eyes would be drawn to the attractive sculptured stonework on the new extension. On close inspection they would discover it was one of the old-time disciples of Bacchus [God of Wine] with a traveller looking on. The disciple is in the act of raising a foaming tankard of ale that has just drawn from the cask at his feet and remarking to the stranger, 'It is in good condition'. The writer concluded, 'An ancient subject with a modern text; the idea must be unique'.

During the next hundred years, the Chetwode would see a great number of minor improvements but nothing to compare with that original conversion. Records clearly indicate that during most of the hundred years this was another pub well-used by the locals for their relaxation purposes. Its popularity continued until well after the Second World War. However, population movements during the 1960s caused a decline in trade. Even then, it never occurred to anyone that one day the Inn might close, never mind be eventually demolished.

The Chetwode Arms, Hightown, 2 Albert Street, c. 1907.

The Chetwode Arms, 2 Albert Streeet (under demolition), c. 1980.

In the late 1970s, a new inner relief road was being planned to cope with the increased traffic using West Street. Highway engineers who needed to complete the West Street extension were convinced that the pub's demolition would not present too many problems. However, in many locals' eyes this monument to the past should never have been demolished. Even its last landlord John Callaghan was convinced it wouldn't be demolished even when given its closing date of 30 April. One month later, in May of 1980 however, it was finally raised to the ground and the road extension was constructed.

During its final days, the figured representation on the chimney that depicted the disciple of Bacchus was carefully removed and remounted above the fireplace of the Victoria Hotel in Victoria Street. Visiting there a few months ago, I discovered it was no longer there and its present whereabouts are unknown. On a more positive note, the mounting stone which had been at the foot of the Chetwode sign (clearly visible on the photograph) was carefully removed and placed in the Jubilee Gardens where, up to the present time, it still remains.

. . . .

For over two hundred years Ye Olde Hostelrie was situated on Hightown almost diagonally opposite the Chetwode. It was one of the few local places that provided stabling facilities within the area. However, it didn't provide any lodging or alcoholic refreshments – they had to be sought elsewhere. The few people who did visit this area probably journeyed between the salt town of Middlewich and the Potteries, obviously a comparatively short journey. Therefore, trade for travellers would be quite rare – what little there was provided by the Church Coppenhall Inns.

The farm absolutely brims with tales from a bygone age, some decades before the railways arrived. I've decided to relate two tales from here. The first concerns the tenant farmer just after the early railway settlers had arrived. The farmer was William Roylance, who settled there in 1847. He was quite a learned man. Earlier in his life he had been parish clerk of Church Coppenhall as well as the village schoolmaster. On taking over the farm, he relinquished all other tasks and began a daily round of delivering milk. He had a passionate addiction to snuff taking, as did many. Every day whilst attending his pails of milk he would be partaking of snuff consequently, whilst filling his pails, he would accidentally speckle the milk with it. It was said by many of his customers, 'it gave the milk the appearance of having cinnamon cast upon it'. Unusually, it may have had the effect of sterilizing the milk for it appears none of his customers suffered from dreaded tuberculosis. This is quite unusual considering that in some parts of the town it was almost epidemic.

My second story from the farm relates to its last inhabitants, three brothers William, Thomas and John Ward who, in 1882, established a horse-drawn omnibus service from there. They provided a service from the George Hotel, West Street via Mill Street to the Royal Hotel. The earliest timetables show ten journeys daily in each direction, with extras on Friday and Saturday. This venture was so successful that by 1901 they were employing enough staff to service five omnibuses, using the Hostelrie for both the stabling of the horses and the headquarters for their business.

Less than ten years later Crewe Corporation decided to form their own horse-drawn fire brigade. It should be realised that until then, the town had been reliant on Railway Co. to provide that service. On its introduction, the Corporation believed it was best if Ward's horses were used to pull the fire appliance. One writer of the time wrote that in

Ye Olde Hostelrie,
Hightown, c. 1910.

the beginning, the idea was quite bizarre. It appears that when the fire bell rang, very often the horses were on their bus duties. This meant they were quickly unharnessed from the bus and were hurriedly sent to the fire station. It seems in those far-off days that whatever passengers were on the bus when that happened, they had to finish their journey on foot. Finally in 1923, because of neglect over many years, the building had become quite unsafe and unfortunately demolition was the only solution.

. . . .

The Oak Farm has, without doubt, had a paramount influence in Crewe history. As early as 1847 the chapel in Exchange Street used its bowling green for their opening ceremony. During its heyday in Victorian times it was extensively used by many of the Vaudeville acts. During these times, this was Crewe's first theatre, until the Lyceum arrived.

However, my tales from the farm's history go back further. Its legendary Steeple Chase, held on the lower pastures of the farm, was held on the second Tuesday in November and the course, straddling the River Waldron, had some jumps. It was always a well-attended competition, people travelling from far and wide. Records show that the most famous Steeple Chaser of them all reputedly was a horse named Bunbury. When he died, he was buried with a fitting ceremony on the slopes overlooking the river Waldron.

In those far-off days, there was also a woodland park running alongside the river with the racecourse naturally using part of it. A writer from 1850 described the area as a delightful sylvan walk used, and fully enjoyed, by the local community. The farmland gently stretched down to the river incorporating both the park and the Steeple Chase course. I imagine it must have been quite picturesque with the Oak Farm standing in its own grounds at the top of the mound with High Street running behind.

This all changed in 1868 with the re-routing of the main line to Chester. Obviously that meant it no longer passed under Chester Bridge but used the new route alongside

The Oak Farm Inn, Oak Street, c. 1958. (The Pioneers Club from 1911-1962.)

the river. This resulted in the building of two new bridges. With the line now diverted, this allowed the Company a facility to build workshops on the triangle of land between the two. This land would be known by generations of railwaymen as the Deviation Works. Right up to the present day, the Chester line has continued to run alongside the river passing under both Edleston Road and Wistaston Road bridges. The downside of the re-routing was it meant the end of both the park and the racecourse.

However idyllic life appeared to be in those far off days, life in Crewe in 1850 was far from idyllic. In fact, they were very difficult times. Most people were employed by the Company working long hours for very little reward. No wonder they turned in ever-increasing numbers to the pub for their relaxation and socializing needs.

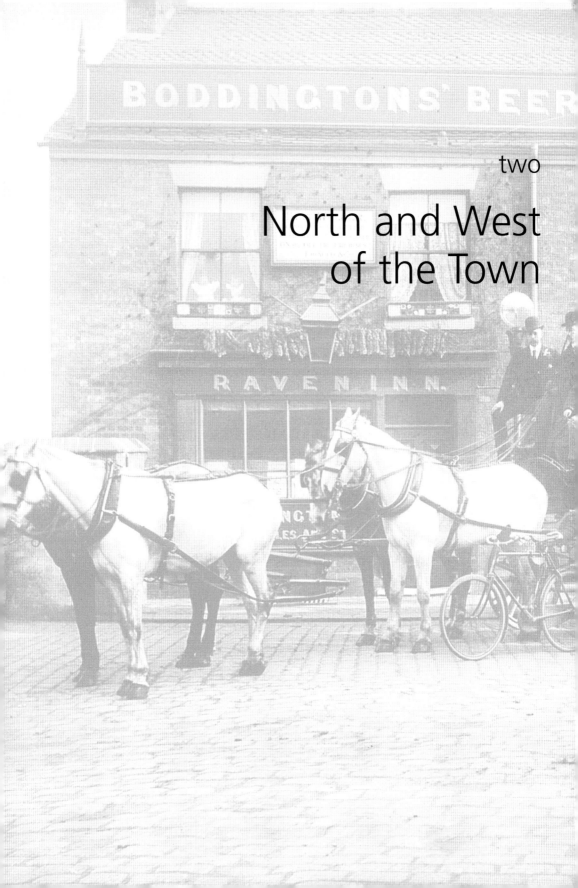

two

North and West of the Town

Cross Keys Hotel, Remer Street, c. 1965.

Cross Green can boast the existence of two Cross Key pubs. To discover that a pub at Cross Green existed before the present pub was built is not too surprising. Church Coppenhall history divulges that before the railways ever thought about settling in the area, Cross Green was one of the best-populated areas within the locality.

Richard Lindop (1778-1871), a local farmer who lived at Maw Green farm, gives an excellent account in his diary of life in this area during the nineteenth century. Although the original pub, a converted farmhouse, dates back to the same period in time, sadly Lindop never mentions this or any other local hostelry.

The rebuilt pub is another good example of late Victorian architecture matching, in design terms, the Royal Hotel and Crewe Arms Hotel. On close inspection it reveals a number of significant highlights, for example a turret doorway with bay windows to match. Its decorative panelling above the door and windows gives it quite an imposing appearance when approached from the North Street side. The building is completed with a striking ornate pitch roof that well designed buildings seem to possess.

The view of Broad Street taken circa 1908 was from roughly outside the former Black Horse Inn. Behind where the Inn stood and beyond the railway line to the north of England was a site of brick-making. It is common knowledge that clay from this part of Coppenhall is ideal for that type of venture. Therefore, it's not surprising to discover that in the past many entrepreneurial brick-makers had operated within that area.

The formation of the Britannia Brick Co. in 1906, with the task of mass-producing bricks, gradually brought about change that and eventually ousted all the smaller firms.

However, this mass producing did have a downside and the clay excavation over the years created a large dangerous pit. In 1967, the Council decided that something needed to be done, as the site had now become a hazard to the general public. As a result, during that year the pit was filled in and the whole area was redeveloped.

In the 1960s, another major change took place, again in Broad Street. The railway bridge changed in structure. All bridges over main lines were significantly altered to accommodate the electrification of the main railway routes. Broad Street Bridge, which had originally been built in 1892, was no exception.

Broad Street, c. 1908.

Bridge Inn, Broad Street, c. 1961.

Spring Tavern,
Broad Street,
c. 1963.

Just off Hightown was another well-known Victorian pub, the Spring Tavern, built c. 1863. Straddling Vere Street and Broad Street, its name was taken from a natural spring situated nearby. The street was originally a cul-de-sac called George Street with the lower reaches named Spring Grove. A 1861 map shows that at the end of the original Spring Grove there was a small wooden footbridge. This footbridge enabled pedestrians to cross the Leighton brook on their way to St. Michael's Church and the surrounding area. Leighton brook is little more than a stream where the bridge crossed it, but has always been the recognized boundary between Monks and Church Coppenhall. It flows for just over five miles through the northern boundary of Monks Coppenhall rising in Sydney and eventually joining the River Weaver at Nantwich. Much of it has now been made into a culvert so very little can be seen of it. The previously mentioned bridge was a few yards from where the present stone gateposts to Brooklands are situated.

The construction of the Cemetery and its opening on 1 January 1872 saw George Street become Cemetery Road. The new name caused the local residents concern. They felt the name 'had one foot in the grave ring about it' and believed another name should have been used. At about the same time as George Street was being renamed, a row of six terraced cottages were being built off it. This small development adopted the name used originally at the bottom end of George Street – that of Spring Grove.

The local residents' 1872 concerns weren't addressed until 1926 when Badger Avenue was under construction. At this stage, the entire street from Hightown to the Cross Keys was renamed Broad Street, and 'Cemetery Road' was discarded. In 1968, the Council's continuing slum clearance programme saw the pub, along with over a hundred houses in this area, being demolished. The land that was created by this clearance was eventually used for Beechwood Primary School.

The Raven, demolished in 1969, transferred its license and its landlord to the new Raven pub, built as its replacement in Brookhouse Drive. Originally built as a house, it was converted in 1863-64 to suit the alcoholic demands of the area. Along with the Harp Inn and the Vernon Arms, it would see to the leisure needs of this community for many

The Raven, Dewes Street,
c. 1897.

The Raven under demolition
c. 1969.

years. As well the usual source of pub entertainment, such as cards and dominoes, a local piano player would regularly play on most weekends. In 1892 however, the local pubs complained at the Licensing Session about what they believed were unfair practices.

Leonard Chambers, Licensee of the Vernon Arms typified how many felt after being refused a singing and music licence by saying, the decision was 'most unfair'. He went on to say, 'It was not English or right that people should be debarred from playing music and singing'. He finished off by saying 'at Nantwich and Sandbach, where this privilege is granted, hundreds flock there at weekends. Obviously that's where our trade is going'. Their complaints made no difference to the Licensing Committee as he, along with all the others, were refused their music licences.

It seemed strange to locals and publicans alike that pubs a few miles away were being granted music licences whilst Crewe pubs were being refused. They perhaps felt that the Temperance movement was exerting some pressure on the local Licensing bench trying to curtail activities in the local pubs.

· ·

The Wolverton Arms built in around 1864 was not a converted house like scores of others, but was a purpose-built pub. It was built at the same time as a Railway Department merge was taking place. This amalgamation resulted in nearly 400 Wolverton railwaymen being transferred to Crewe, 700 people in total when their families are taken into account. All had to be housed in the vicinity of the Company's works. Most would settle in West Street and the surrounding areas of Alexander, Grosvenor and Naylor Streets. Whilst this influx was happening, a new pub was being built on the corner of Alexander Street. It was named Wolverton Arms so as to attract the latest newcomers.

As the pub was nicknamed 'The Monkey' for more years than most residents can remember, the present owner has officially renamed it The Monkey. There are various possibilities as to why it became known as this in the first instance. The first tenant

The Wolverton Arms, West Street, c. 1920.

landlord reputedly owned a chimpanzee that sat on the bar, gibbering away at his customers. Another possibility can be found in the workmen themselves. When the 400 railwaymen were transferred from Wolverton, they were employed in the Company's works. The Crewe artisans felt the newcomers were taking the better-paid jobs, and accused them of pinching work like a 'load of monkeys'. The Wolverton men met in their pub, which became known to the locals as The Monkey. We will probably never know if either theories are correct, but both seem plausible.

In the early part of the twentieth century, Ezra Nixon owned the shop next to the Wolverton Arms. He was a local councillor and was Mayor in 1925. Ezra was an idiosyncratic character − a personality so unusual that tales of his exploits have reverberated around the West End for many years. In the opinion of most locals, 'The West End is the Best End' has become his most lasting and endearing phrase.

. . . .

History does not fully acknowledge the importance of the Railway Company to the early Bessemer process of making steel. Sir Henry Bessemer invented this new process of steel-making in 1856, and quickly convinced the LNWR Company of its benefits. Due to the success of the world's first steel railway lines at Crewe Station in November 1861, it was decided to open a steel-making plant west of Flag Lane by 1864. For this to happen, the Bessemer Vaults constructed on the corner of Bessemer Street (Richard Moon Street) and Hill Street West (Goddard Street.) had to be demolished. That allowed

The Company's Entrance, Goddard Street, c. 1960.

The Bessemer Hotel, Richard Moon Street, c. 1965.

the Company to not only extend their works but to contemplate a new Goddard Street entrance.

The new Hotel and the redesigned Goddard Street entrance were opened in 1874. They served each other's purposes for well over fifty years. During that period, a great number of apprentices hurried through the gates and onto the pub to get their beer. For many years, the necessity of a drink was explained by the dry, arid conditions of the Bessemer plant, the forges, melting pits and foundries. Hence the workers were allocated a small beer ration that apprentices collected for them using a token system. To ensure the men's needs were met, the pub even had a twenty-four-hour licence at one time.

The Bessemer Hotel, steeped in local history and home of hundreds of steel-maker's memories was sadly demolished without any ceremony in March 1980.

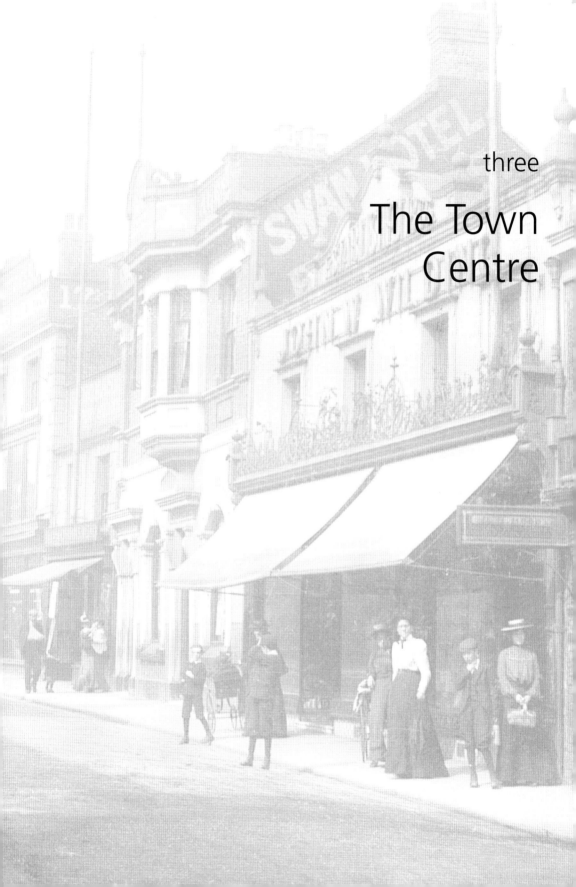

three

The Town
Centre

Adelphi Hotel, Market Street, c. 1958.

The Adelphi Hotel was one of the town's original thirteen hotels, inns and taverns. It was built and opened in late 1843, and was reputedly named by the construction workers who, feeling homesick, named it after a well-known Hotel in Liverpool. Some past residents have argued that it was possibly the first building to be constructed in Small Lane (Earle Street) although others argue that the town's first Methodist Chapel takes that honour. The chapel, on the site of the present Municipal Buildings, was officially opened in October 1843 about a month before the Adelphi.

Two years later, in 1845, the Mechanic's Institute, better known as the Town Hall, was erected opposite the Chapel. 1852 saw the first Catholic Church being built that on the site of the present Lyceum Theatre; in 1854, John Hill, a well-known railway contractor, built the Market Hall. The Market Tavern, a pub converted from a cottage, then opened in 1848; it was situated between the chapel and the Market Hall. Four years later in 1852 another pub, the Forester's Arms, opened further along the street. It was not a long-term success however, as after lying derelict for some time, it was turned into a suite of offices for the Council in 1893.

In 1902 the Adelphi Hotel was planning to add twenty bedrooms using property next-door to them in Earle Street. However, because of the brewery's uncertainty, this never happened. After 118 years of trading, the Adelphi regretfully closed and was replaced by another modern development. For over fifty years, the wealth of shops, pubs and cafés had made this corner of Market/Earle Street the hub of Crewe life. Crewe residents now generally believe that the design of those buildings fitted in with the street scene much more than their modern counterparts.

The town's original thirteen hotels and inns were supported by eight beer houses which catered for the alcoholic requirements of Crewe's population of nearly 5,000. However, when the first railway workers were transferred from Edge Hill in 1843, only one of the new pubs was ready to deal with their requirements.

The Company was obviously building the new town around its works. Christ Church and its surrounding streets were the centre of the estate bound by Earle Street in the north, Lyon Street in the east, Forge Street to the south, Betley, Dorfold and Tollit streets and the cul-de-sac of Delamere Street with Victoria Street as far as Hightown in the west. The main streets from the railway station to the new settlement were along Nantwich Road and via Mill Street, Coppenhall Terrace and Earle Street.

Along these streets the first pubs would begin to spring up and they would be the heart of the town's entertainment for many years to come. The owners and tenants would rapidly change, but it is perhaps important to remember those who initially ran these pubs. The Bridge Tavern and the White Bear were furthermore almost opposite each other on the other side of the north of England line. Soon after the first railway workers had been transferred consideration was given by the Company to building a small halt nearer the town centre. Strong rumours suggest that an early entrepreneur overheard this plan and built pubs in readiness for the trade that the halt might bring.

The Adelphi, Earle Street. (Agent Mr James Grace)
Bridge Tavern, Small Lane. (now Earle St.) (Tenant Mr John Vernon)
Crewe Arms, Nantwich Road. (Landlord Mr William Edwards)
Grand Junction, Victoria Street. (Landlord Mr Thomas Dale)
Red Bull, Market Street. (Tenant Mr Thomas Moss)
Royal Oak, High Street. (Landlord Mr Charles Hyde)
White Bear, Earle Street. (Tenant Mr William Sherratt)
Blue Cap Dog, Market Street. (Tenant Mrs Mary Monday)
Commercial, Oak Street. (Tenant Mr Samuel McGeorge)
Egerton Arms, Nantwich Road. (Tenant Mr Henry Horrabin)
Oak Farm Inn, Oak Street. (Landlord Mr John Pointon)
Royal Hotel, Nantwich Road. (Tenant Mrs Jane Silvester)
Swan Inn, Victoria Street. (Tenant Mrs Mary Jinks)

These thirteen were supported by eight beerhouses: two in Nantwich Road, two in High Street, two in Mill Street and one each in Victoria Street and Earle Street. Some interesting names begin to appear within these early beerhouses, The Robin Hood, The Globe, The Neptune, Dog and Partridge, and the Market Tavern. To complete this picture of pubs, a further four were right on the outskirts of the new settlement those being the Blue Bell Inn in Sandy Lane (now Broad Street), the Horse Shoe in North Street, The George in Lower Nantwich Road (now West Street) and the Cross Keys at Cross Green. Therefore, in 1850, the area that eventually became Crewe had seventeen Hotels and Inns supported by no less than ten beerhouses.

. . . .

Crewe was typical of an industrial town in that the family home was small and totally unsuitable for any kind of social activity without disrupting the whole household. Most homes, as many of you are well aware, were very small indeed. In many instances, they

Moss Square (on the right is the wall around Christ Church), c. 1958.

were two-up and two-down with the usual out houses at the bottom of the garden. Consequently the pub was the best option for relaxation for the working man.

From 1842 until 1848, some 520 houses were built covering an area of about thirty acres. This became the nucleus of the earlier railway colony. The houses of Coppenhall Terrace, Chester, Delamere, Dorfold, Betley and Tollit Streets were, from all accounts, increased by development in the Christ Church area from 1843-44. These houses would provide customers for pubs built on their peripheries. There is undisputed evidence that the clay from the excavations of the original church was used for the construction of most of the houses in this area. A local brick-maker named John Bunting, with kilns in Russell Street (now Heath Street), used the excavated clay for the making of bricks. They were then sold to the Company for use of the building of their houses around the church.

In 1887 the *Crewe Guardian* made the following observation of the town: 'Crewe is essentially a working man's town, men who are accustomed to working all day in the forge, at the furnaces, or at the rolling mill. Therefore, there is little pleasure for them in the admiration of architectural beauty'. It concluded, 'The standard of education for the majority of the working class was not conductive for cultural pastimes. Consequently it's not surprising that men visited the pub for relaxation and escapism'.

The Guardian addressed the situation in Crewe in 1887 by commenting how men whose daily work was physically hard needed relaxation of the simplest kind. Whilst, the pub did not apply to everyone, it appealed to a large majority.

The Grand Junction Hotel was constructed during February and March 1844. It was obviously named after the Railway Company whose workforce had recently been

The Grand Junction Hotel, Victoria Street, c. 1927.

transferred to Crewe. Less than eighteen months later there was a buzz of excitement around the town when it was announced that the Company was merging with various other railway companies. The new enlarged one would become the London North Western Railway Company, a name synonymous with engineering skills the length and breadth of England. In 1923, the Company became the London Midland and Scottish and in 1948 it then became British Railways. Although the name had changed over the years, Railway Company Works at Crewe remained the envy of the world for its engineering prowess.

Crewe continues to have a pub named the Grand Junction but it has moved from its original site. During the redevelopment of Market Street in 1984, the pub was demolished and rebuilt on the site of the former Empire Cinema in Heath Street. However, the sign outside now displays a rival company's locomotive!

The Swan Hotel, locally known as the Big Duck, was built in late 1846 and demolished in 1968. It was one of the original thirteen, but in the beginning was named the Swan Inn. It is probably best remembered by the local populace in that it offered its customers the use of a full-sized snooker table. Once again, this emphasizes the pub's role in providing differing leisure pursuits. Looking towards Hightown, the sign outside the Angel is quite visible, whilst further on up Victoria Street, the outline of the Star is just about discernible.

The Burton Hotel was built in 1862 on land next to the Baptist Chapel which had been built two years before. The pub's first name was Union Inn but it changed to Burton Hotel in 1873. This coincides with the opening of another a well-known beerhouse, The Staffordshire Knot. That particular beer house was on the opposite side

VICTORIA ST CREWE. 373-2

and lower down the street, by Lawrence Street. Although Victoria Street is a comparatively short street, it is the main road from the west of the town and has always been one of the town's more densely populated pub areas, rivalled perhaps only by Mill Street.

· ·

As the population continued to grow, the land north of Delamere Street was developed. Fitting neatly behind the already-built Market Terrace were Sandbach, Charles and Lawrence Streets. Both the latter were named in honour of Dr Charles Lawrence, a Director of the Grand Junction Railway Co.

No less than twenty pubs were in a half-mile radius of the new houses, seven of the twenty in Victoria Street. The Star Hotel, pictured at the far end of Lawrence Street, was one of those seven. There were no pubs inside the housing complex. Perhaps this was part of the Company's policy, or simply for better trading.

A quite remarkable story has emerged from the building of these houses. Not only were the bricks made by the Company, but the mortar they used was a bit special.

Opposite above
Swan Hotel,
Victoria Street.
c. 1907.

Opposite below
The Burton Hotel,
Victoria Street.
c. 1922.

Above right
Lawrence Street.
c. 1954.

Below right
Charles Street.
c. 1956.

During the mixing of the mortar, sand was used from the iron foundry. This sand contained miniscule pieces of metal. Furthermore, according to local records, instead of using water during the mixing, they used an Oxen's blood. Not only were the cottages well-designed, therefore, but they were also extremely robust in repelling the most inclement of weather. On demolition from 1958-59, the strength of these houses was more than apparent in the Herculean effort that was needed to demolish them.

· ·

Around this time there was also a phenomenal rise in clubs in Victorian Crewe. The Liberals established their first club in 1878 on the corner of Maxwell Street and Edleston Road. When a new club was planned, they decided to seek a different location and eventually acquired a site in Gatefield Street; the new club opened there on 5 December 1901. Since then, whilst its interior has seen many alterations, the exterior is almost the same as when first constructed with the only noticeable difference being that a hundred years ago it had skylight windows.

When the Conservatives came into power in 1890, they used a house in Beech Street as their quarters before moving to Victoria Street. The Unionists opened their first club in 1896 from a house in Beech Street. Clubs from these early political beginnings prospered quite astonishingly. By 1922 there were seventeen registered clubs with membership of over 7,000 within the town. Clubs had without a doubt become another

LIBERAL CLUB,

The Liberal Club, Gatefield Street, c. 1902.

The Conservative
Club, Victoria
Street, c. 1964.

source of providing the local residents with entertainment and a meeting place. This boom in clubs was really more than them providing better facilities; it was undoubtedly their ability to sell cheaper drinks.

History shows conclusively that the railwaymen of Crewe had a sense of their own respectability and were self-disciplined accordingly. The majority knew that railway work demanded sober workers. As such, they were not given the chance to become heavy drinkers. Problems of heavy drinking which other industrial areas suffered never took hold in Crewe. When trouble with drink threatened to become a problem, the Company took action.

The action was often severe. In a 1869 incident, a Crewe foreman committed suicide after being sacked by the Company for drunken behaviour. The Crewe Guardian commented, 'Crewe is an exceptional place to live, the population is totally dependant on the Directors of the Company for their livelihood and anyone who strays from that belief must suffer the consequences". The local populace didn't need reminding to whom they owed their living, and the occasional dismissal for a drink problem would undoubtedly have brought the exceptions back into line.

Company employment was extremely hard work, with a working week of sixty-two hours Monday to Saturday. On Sunday, they attended church. Working on the Permanent Way was no less demanding and in many instances was quite the opposite. Engine drivers' and firemens' tasks were equally laborious; all round, the Crewe's railwaymen had a pretty bleak life. A leading writer of the time concluded, 'hobbies and relaxation were that of totally exhausted men'. The pubs endeavoured to provide a relaxing, comfortable niche..

The range of activities and functions within the pub's scope was quite extraordinary. They provided the only meeting place for the many clubs and societies that prevailed in the area. Good examples of this can be found in the minutes of organisations. The Crewe Angling Society No. 1, for instance, met at the Old Vaults in High Street whilst the

Albert Hotel, Oakley Steet, *c.* 1972.

No. 2 society met on a regular basis at the Albert Hotel. Even the most serious aspects of life were held within public house walls; most inquests were held in a local pub, for example. Perhaps it was because they had the only available rooms or maybe the local magistrate fancied a tipple after the proceedings! Whatever the reasons, it was normal procedure for inquests to be held in a pub. Public houses therefore acted as a meeting place, and as some modern-thinking historians have pointed out, played a similar role to the present day Community Centre.

The Spread Eagle was reputedly the smallest bar in the whole of England, and a few years ago was in the *Guinness Book of Records* for that reason. It first appeared in records in 1873 as another Victorian-created front-room pub. After just over a hundred years of existence, it was demolished as part of the Council's continued slum-clearance policy.

That it existed for one hundred years is amazing as it was in danger of closing at the turn of the twentieth century. There were vast numbers of other pubs in the locality making it, according to the brewery, economically non-viable. The Brewery wanted to close the Spread Eagle along with a number of other locals in an effort cut costs. At the time, a brewery could apply for compensation for the loss of trade by the closure of a pub. After much wrangling, however, they were unsuccessful in their application, and it was decided that the Spread Eagle should carry on with the business.

The Spread Eagle was located on Ludford Street. Landowner Sir John Chetwode Bart owned most of the land in this area. The Company had the responsibility for street-naming during house-building in this locality and decided to use his name for the streets

Right Spread Eagle, Ludford Street, *c.* 1968.

Below Star Inn, Victoria Street, *c.* 1972.

in this area. Two were subsequently named John and Chetwode, then his middle names, the others Newdigate and Ludford. Finally, they referred to the family home, at Oakley Hall in Staffordshire. That a landlord who probably never visited the district had these five streets named in his honour is quite remarkable!

Angel Hotel, Victoria Street, c. 1965.

Mid-Victorian Crewe saw many pubs in multi-purpose use. In 1874, Harry Hill, a blacksmith, rented the Angel's yard to shoe horses. It was a successful combination. Whilst a horse was having the necessary treatment the owner, often a local farmer, called into the pub to enjoy a drink. The blacksmith did not just deal with the farmer. There were great numbers of workhorses that needed constant attention.

Horses were intrinsic to successful business during this era. A report from the September 1913 Council minutes said: 'Alderman Kettell asked if consideration could be given to the question of providing four half-legged horses for the Fire Engine. "Furthermore", he continued, "could future consideration be given to exchanging the present horse-drawn Steam Fire Engine for a motor-driven Steamer".' A half-legged horse was a cross between a Thoroughbred and a Shire.

After just over a century of existence, the Angel, a well-known landmark as well as a bus stop, was demolished. During the mid 1980s, the redevelopment of the area saw its site become occupied by a well-known Building Society. As a result of this development, the Angel became relocated underneath it; sadly, despite having been a vital ingredient to the community, the pub is now no longer visible to the local populace.

. . . .

The Rifleman and the Beech Tree were situated on opposite sides of Beech Street, a cobbled street that joined Hightown to Market Street. The street had been named after Thomas Beech, a well-known farmer who had lived at Hillock House on Hightown, now the site of the Jubilee Gardens. As older residents will remember, Beech Street was a Victorian street that ran through an estate of over a thousand houses and linked Hightown with Market Street.

As previously mentioned, in Edwardian times, horses for the Corporation Fire Brigade were stabled at Ye Olde Hostelrie on Hightown. The Fire Station was at the lower end of a steep hill in Beech Street East. When the fire bell tolled, the sight of horses briskly trotting down this cobbled street to the fire station was quite something. Invariably, because of the steep incline, they would slip on the cobbled street and sparks would fly from their hooves as the handlers tried to control them.

Eventually this became another area that was part of the Council's ongoing slum-clearance programme. In 1969, houses in Beech Street and adjoining streets were demolished, as well as these two pubs. By 1974, the programme was complete.

Beech Tree Inn, Beech Street, c. 1971.

The Rifleman, Beech Street, c. 1973.

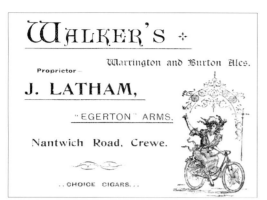

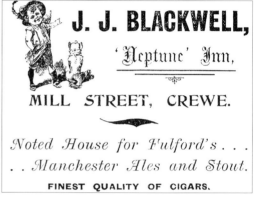

Victorian pub adverts, c. 1895.

Towards the end of the nineteenth century, pubs attempted to attract more customers through advertisements. Those shown above were all extracted from local press articles dated late 1895 and illustrate the competitiveness. Note how artistically they present their product.

. . . .

The collection (*opposite*) of Crewe pub advertisements are from early Edwardian days. These were extracted from press articles in 1908. They show the many varied attractions local pubs were prepared to stage. It appears that every pastime and game imaginable was commonplace in most pubs.

Local Edwardian adverts, c. 1908.

River Waldron flowing past Woolf's Millwheel, *c.* 1927.

In just over twenty-five years since the first railways workers arrived, the town's population had grown to somewhere around 30,000. There was subsequently a significant increase in the number of pubs. Breweries and local businessmen grasped the commercial opportunities this boom presented. Within the brewery business, the most daring enterprise of the day was the established by E.S. Woolf in the late 1850s. He established Crewe's first and only brewery, built in Wistaston Road, trading under the name of the South Cheshire Brewery Co. Built on vacant land on the corner of Walthall Street and Wistaston Road, it covered around five acres, stretching down to the river Waldron (Valley Brook). The mill wheel was, in fact, driven by the flowing waters of the river.

In 1860, a pub was built on the periphery of the land, on the corner of Walthall Steet. The Broughton Arms officially opened later that year. Just over twenty-five years later, it became the Queens Park Hotel in celebration of the official opening of Queens Park. The Hotel unsurprisingly sold Woolf's beer. It was reputed that the beer was made from the splendid waters of the River Waldron.

The brewery flourished quite significantly during its early years, but by the turn of the twentieth century had started to decline and finally closed in 1923. In its heyday, the brewery served the requirements of only eight local hotels and eleven local beerhouses, less than a third of the town's drinking establishments. It never ventured very far afield for its business and the Cross Keys appears to be its only outlet away from the main town.

As late as the mid-1950s, remnants of the dam and mill could still be seen. Many local people can remember parts of the old brewery being used as a bottling plant in the late 1960s. Browns' bottling plant ran parallel with old Duke Street with the main office, a two-storey building, situated in Wistaston Road. Two large wooden gates were the entrance and exit of the brewery, most of which was cobble-stoned. The millwheel and the dam were totally demolished in 1964. That finally obliterated all traces of Crewe's only brewery.

River Waldron 'meandering' past Flag Lane, c. 1904.

This 1904 scene from Alton Street looks over the River Waldron and up the cul-de-sac of Flag Lane. This dead-end street caused a number of problems over the years. In March 1913, the Town clerk reported to a Council committee that 'whilst riding down Flag Lane, people could see the streetlights of Alton Street. Far too many of them who were not familiar with the area thought it was a 'through road'. He concluded his report by saying 'a few had realised their mistake almost too late and had nearly gone into the river'. He suggested to the committee that 'to stop cyclists etc. inadvertently riding down Flag Lane and into the river, an illuminated sign should be erected warning of the danger'. This was agreed and later that year a sign was erected warning of the dangers on the corner of Wistaston Road and Flag Lane by the Earl of Chester. That sign stayed in existence for just over ten years until the bridge over the river was finally built.

The bridge solved both this and other problems. Although discussed for a number of years, it was finally agreed that the housing development south of the town needed better access into town. The bridge was greatly needed especially for anyone employed in the Company's Works. Local residents had previously used an old wooden bridge that was situated a short distance upstream. Although it is no longer wooden, a bridge still crosses the same spot today. A local said: 'a river crossing at this point is older than Crewe itself'.

Residents from the west of Alton Street area gained access into town via the Stewart Street Bridge. Most of the road traffic from Nantwich used Walthall Street, this being a main thoroughfare during mid-Victorian times. A large roundabout on the corner of Walthall and Alton Street dealt with the vast amount of horse-drawn traffic arriving from the south.

Eventually the desire for a new bridge became imperative for easier access into town. The river was realigned and a bridge was constructed. It was officially opened in November 1923. The land on the left of the photograph was owned by the Richard Edleston trust. The land on either side of the river was bought from the Trustees by the Council in 1924. Valley Park was then constructed and following that, on the slope towards the river, the Swimming Baths were built. These were officially opened on 6 November 1937 by the Mayor of Crewe, Alderman Frank Bott.

Astonishingly, Wistaston Road has been home to seven pubs and one brewery during its comparatively short history. The pubs are: the Duke of Bridgewater, Queens Park Hotel, the Stag, Ireland Green, Parkers Vaults, the Earl of Chester and Hop Pole Hotel.

· ·

For many years, most locals believed a pub named the Island Green was on the corner of Flag Lane and Wistaston Road. The assumption is wrong; its official address was 91 Wistaston Road, the other end of the row of terraced houses and by the gully linking Flag Lane Bridge with Alton Street. Locals argue that this gully was used by monks on the way from the mill in Mill Lane to St Michael's Church. It's reasonable to assume that by using a bridge or stepping-stones over the river Waldron they were able to make quicker progress to the church.

The Island Green is another pub with a very short existence. Although it was a beerhouse in 1874, a couple of years later it had ceased trading and become a corner shop. It is also

The site of the former Ireland Green, Wistaston Rd, 2003.

The site of the former Parkers Vaults, Wistaston Rd, 2003.

likely that its name was incorrectly interpreted. As large numbers of Irish immigrants took up residence in the area, its name is more likely to have been Ireland Green.

The misunderstanding seems to have arisen with the existence of the beer retailer on the corner of Flag Lane in around 1873. It seems the property was called Parkers Vaults, but this is not certain due to the bad record-keeping and the number of beerhouses that opened and closed within months. The Parkers Vault was a small front room pub which five years later was a corner shop selling everything including beer.

. . . .

The closure of Parkers Vault almost coincides with the building of The Earl of Chester's Own, on the opposite corner of Wistaston Road and Flag Lane. It was built as a beerhouse but also provided stabling facilities and overnight accommodation. It was quite unusual for this type of property, and the facility was not well-used. Landlords nevertheless tried to encourage more customers as times were precarious. A lack of customers caused many local pubs to be sold by public auction for instance, the Anchor Inn in Mill Street, the Talbot Inn and the Vernon Arms (both in Stafford Street).

A notice of an auction of a well-known beerhouse appeared in the *Crewe Guardian* on the 29 June 1872. It reads, 'To Brewers and Innkeepers. Mr Hill has been favoured with instructions from Mr Brereton to offer for public competition on Monday 22 July, at 6p.m. at the Royal Hotel Crewe, the aforesaid; the newly and substantially built Beerhouse, situated in Mill Street. Having two frontages, with vaults, live down stair rooms, seven bedrooms, excellent cellaring, stables and coach house'. This was the Albion Inn in Mill Street.

In a 1936 endeavour to raise much-needed funds for Webb's Orphanage, an appeal was launched in the town. The Orphanage had been built through the £70,000 bequeathed in the will of Francis William Webb, but was having great difficulty in raising enough money to keep it fully functional. The year 1936 was the centenary of Webb's birth and a number of leading citizens thought it should be celebrated. Local businesses and hoteliers gave it their full support, and a grand draw was organized. The tickets were priced at 6d, with 160 main prizes being organized. The first prize was a magnificent four-foot bedroom walnut suite with a value of twenty-five guineas, presented by Mr John Leach. The second prize, which was offered by Mr J. Grosvenor, the Earl of Chester's landlord, was, 'A bottle of Stout or Beer every night for three months' or, if the winner was female, 'half a dozen

Earl of Chester,
Wistaston Rd.
c. 1989.

pairs of silk stockings and a pair of pink suspenders. If a teetotaller was to win, 'a magnum of Epsom Salts or any other cold and cheerless drink' was awarded, but it was not to be drunk in the company of Mr Grosvenor.

· ·

Another pub enhanced its popularity with the creation of a bowling green. The Hop Pole Hotel in Wistaston Road followed the lead that had been set by the Oak Farm Inn, and created a green for the enjoyment of its customers. Over a number of years it has served the local bowling fraternity with many hours of entertainment and enjoyment. The space was not used simply as a bowling green, but was also enjoyed by a number of dancing troops.

The dancing troop, Promenade Dancers, are seen here practising on the Hop Pole's green in the very early 1920s and were just one of many groups to do so. According to the Brass Shop, this particular troop consisted of men from Crewe works; even the women places are taken up by men. This serves as another good example of a pub serving the needs of the local community.

Above The Hop Pole, Wistaston Road, c. 1989.

Left Promenade dancers, Hop Pole Bowling Green, c. 1922.

The photograph of the troop was taken just before the Valley Park and Flag Lane bridge was built. At this time, access from the houses in the background – Vinegar Hill – to this pub was difficult. There are no real leads as to why this unusual nickname was adopted. There are a couple of unsubstantiated theories from the locals but nothing that seriously attempts to solve the riddle. It remains a piece of local history that has been lost in the passage of time.

The Amazon Lancers were another troop to grace the Hop Pole green with their expertise, this time as part of the Hospital Fête. Many of these troops were made up of men from different railway departments. Their competitors were the all-female troops from the many different clothing factories. All took great delight in taking part, helping to raise money for the local Cottage Hospital and hoping to win a prize at the same time.

The honour for the most unusual prize in any of the local fêtes held over the years should be awarded to a winner in the 1901 Patriotic Carnival. This particular fête was

Above Amazon Lancers, Hop Pole Bowling Green, c. 1924.

Right Extract from the Patriotic Carnival Programme, c. 1901.

PRIZE LIST.

Prize.	Given by.	No. of Prizes.	Section given to.
1 Box (500) Ogden's Cigarettes Firkin of Beer, value 14/-	Ogden's Guinea Gold Co., Liverpool Dixon & Co., Hanley	1st	Best Workshop Section
1 Box of Choice Cigars, value 5 - 1 Bottle of Whiskey, value 4/6 A Prize, value 5/-	Mr. Howard, "Victoria" Hotel Mr. Vickers, "Engine" Inn Mr. Hillier, Earle Street	2nd	Ditto
1 Box of Cigars 1 Silver-mounted Pipe, value 5/-	Mr. Hamilton, "Duke of Bridgw'r" Inn Mr. Vernon, Hightown	3rd	Ditto
1 Box of Cigars 1 Pipe, value 2/6	Mr. Parry, "Beech-Tree" Inn Mr. Ward, West Street	4th	Ditto
1 Box of Cigars 1 Gent's Muffler	Mr. Jones, "Jubilee" Tavern	5th	Ditto
1 Bottle of Whiskey	Mr. Ellam, "Burton" Hotel	6th	Ditto

Judges:— W. Astle, Stockport ; Wallace Lumb, J.P. ; Councillor Jervis, Dr. Gray.
Judging to take place Market Street and Coppenhall Terrace.

Prize.	Given by.	No. of Prizes.	Section given to.
1 Set of False Teeth, value £6 6s.	Mr. Harris, Mill Street	1st	To the neatest and most artistically dressed lady in any section. If not required by winner can be given to any of her friends

47

held at Crewe Hall to raise funds for the Volunteer & Reservist Memorial Fund. The prize list to which many local businesses and Licensed Victuallers had contributed was quite extensive. There were over fifty prizes for different sections within the parade. The *pièce de resistance* is on page twelve of the programme and reads as follows: 'To the neatest and most artistically dressed lady in any section would be awarded the prize of a set of false teeth. If not required by the winner, this could be given to one of her friends'.

Whilst looking at a couple of the troupes that previously used the Hop Pole bowling green, it should not be overlooked that most of the town's pubs were used as rehearsal venues. Crewe's fête had become regarded as one of the best around, perhaps because of the element of competition existing between railway departments and clothing factories. This rivalry extended to almost all leisure activities including darts, dominoes, football, cricket etc, but cumulating with the fête.

This type of rivalry is summed up quite exceptionally with a monologue, written by Jim Lovatt a few years ago. Included because of the influence the dancing troupes had on Crewe's social history, it is a worthy inclusion despite its poetic licence.

Those Were The Days

On a hot summer day, some years ago
At the North Shed, they had a debate
It was not about work, or double trip jobs
Or what caused some trains to run late.

It was a meeting of firemen and drivers
To discuss the Park Fête on the spot
As George Pidcock said 'we've got to join in
Whether we like it or not'.

We've been Artists and Models, and
    Crimson Hussars.
Dutch Dancers, Toy Soldiers too
But this year, it's going to be different
And it's all up to me and you.

We've not won the trophy for ages
But this year I've made special plans
You're going to be Japanese Dancers
So get practising flirting your fans.

It will take a concerted effort
And demand the best that we've got
'Cos apart from the winning the trophy
We've got to beat Rattigan's lot'.

We're going into serious training
And some of you had better start slimming
'Cos you big blokes will be alright as fellows
But, you little uns are going to be women'.

So, they started to practise in earnest
And soon they were at it like fury
Three nights every week rehearsing the dance
To a cornet played by Dan Drury.

The rest of the band brought their trumpets along
And things were beginning to hum
Bill Thorley, Sam Cooper, and Bob Lewis were there
And Tubby Skellern – he played the big drum.

They had beautiful costumes in Japanese style
With pigtails that hung at the rear
The lads that were wenches, had kimonos of silk
And a Chrysanthemum stuck in each ear

At the final rehearsal 'any questions' it was asked
And one chap asked on the spot
'When I'm doing the dance-what do I do with the
    fan?'
You'll not be surprised at the answer he got.

The Co-op Band performing as the Bumpo Royal Circus of Varieties, c. 1923

At last came the day they'd all worked for
The sun shone down with great heat
The procession assembled at one o'clock sharp
At the playground in Westminster Street.

There were Jazz & Pipe Bands, & all sorts of Troupes
And Doody's girls all in their gear
A group of Crewe Alex supporters were there
But they'd only come for the beer.

There were bicycles dressed like Pagodas
And Sailor girls all dressed in blue
But there was no sign of the Japanese Dancers
But of course the pubs didn't shut till Two.

The Mayor, he was there in a horse-drawn Landau
And the Carnival Queen all in silk
Some of the cream of society were there
And some that were more like sour milk.

The people all cheered as they marched down the street
With the big drummer banging his drum
He kept up his strength, with tablets of yeast
And sips from a bottle of rum.

Now to play the big drum was no easy task
And soon he was puffing and blowing
And to make matters worse, with the drum on his chest
He couldn't see where is was going.

Down Edleston Road there were buntings and flags
There were thousands lining the street
They had climbed up the lamp posts & on the roof tops
And everyone thought it a treat.

All went quite well till Burton's corner was reached
And the bottle of rum almost gone
The procession turned left up Victoria Street
But the big drummer – he kept straight on.

He kept banging away with his Pom tiddley Pom
When suddenly he missed all his mates
He put down the drum and took a look round
And found he was inside the Cemetery gates.

Now the buses in those days, were not like are now
Not nearly so frequent or quick
They trundled along at ten miles an hour
On solid tyres, three inches thick.

'Toreadors', Westminster Street, c. 1924.

The fare was a penny in those far off days
Which then, was quite a large sum
So that's what they charged him - a penny for him
And one and six for the drum.

When they reached Merrill's bridge the procession
    had gone
But there was further trouble in store
For the passengers couldn't get off or on
For the drum had become stuck in the door.

They pushed and they pulled, but it just wouldn't
    budge
And the crowd on the bus were beginning to mutter
So, they sent for the Shed's Breakdown Gang
To bring an Oxy - Acetylene cutter.

Six hours it took, to get that drum free
And the bus driver kicked up a fuss
Which wasn't very surprising to me
For they'd cut off - the top half of his bus.

It had gone quite dark when they got to the park
Which was all lit up with candles and rushes
There were Japanese Dancers dashing all round
The place chasing Doody's girls into the bushes.

The Mayor had gone home, and so had the troupes
And the dancing was over I fear
And so is this story - for I never found out
Who did win the trophy that year?

Another monologue I have been privileged to read was discovered in an old soldier's possessions a few years ago. I feel it sums up superbly what many of our Armed Forces thought about whilst serving abroad. Frank Millward carried this with him for many years probably not knowing who wrote it. Nevertheless everyone's roots are laid somewhere, and Frank's were obviously very firmly with Crewe. For him and no doubt countless numbers of others away from home, this brought back many happy memories.

Unfortunately, when I was given the document it had been folded away in his pocket for a number of years. I was not therefore able to decipher it all. However, there is enough for anyone to get a general idea of its content which is, incidentally, copied exactly word-for-word as it was written.

Dame Horner's Dream of Crewe

I dreamt I was seized by a strong pair of CUMBERLAND ARMS and lifted onto the footplate of the STEAM ENGINE. Where I found BRUNEL and BESSEMER, who had driven through the BURTON Steps with a COACH and HORSES called the BRITISH LION. The panels of the coach bearing respectively the CREWE ARMS and the EGERTON ARMS, which were BARREL-shaped.

As we hurried along the RAILWAY I saw the QUEENS ARMS thrown up in horror for, the WHITE LION was disturbed by the sound of a BLUE BELL. The RAVEN moved and flew straight into the MASONIC ARMS, which was protected by a RIFLEMAN from the VERNON ARMS.

As we rushed at EXPRESS speed past the JUNCTION a CANNON was fired from the ISLAND GREEN, which, so terrified an ANGEL from the MARKET INN that she stumbled over a HOP POLE. She would have fallen into the OLD VAULTS but, for the BOILERMAKERS ARMS who dropped the GLOBE, NEPTUNE had been kicking. Just then the SPREAD EAGLE rushed below to find the ANCHOR, which had been, painted BRUNSWICK black like the NEW INN.

LORD RAGLAN stooped and picked up a STAG, which had, fell from the IMPERIAL CROWN and, rushed with it to the CASTLE. Where the DOG from the BOROUGH ARMS sat at the ROYAL entrance guarding VICTORIA and ALBERT who, with the PRINCE of WALES were admiring a fine BULLS HEAD in the KINGS ARMS. Close at hand in the MONKEY, which bore the WOLVERTON ARMS. I espied a maiden gently strumming the strings of a HARP who had just regaled herself with honey from a BEEHIVE. The DUKE of BRIDGEWATER inquired whether I had been into the CHEESE HALL and asked the ADELPHI from the UNION where the men for the ALBION had been found.

The STIRLING TAP was running the TALBOT closely in the QUEENS PARK Plate and as they passed the ROCKWOOD it concealed the STAG, LION and SWAN gossiping to the GEORGE and DRAGON under the branches of a LABURNUM.

The RISING SUN shone brightly in the face of ROBIN HOOD as he planted a VINE at the OAK FARM. Before that he took a COMFORTABLE GILL with Mrs Astley whose, BIG DUCK had stolen the NAGS HEAD out of the FORESTERS ARMS. Who was taking it to GEORGE who was staying at the BELLE VUE.
Then I was awakened by the musical strains of the Salvation Army's big drum and, found to my disappointment it was all a dream.

H.T.

The passage prompts a number of questions, for instance, who was Dame Horner? Who do the initials H.T. belong to? What do they mean? Can anyone shed some light on the piece? Does anyone have a copy of the full and unabridged version?

View from the roof of Dane Bank College, c. 1982.

The panoramic view of Crewe was taken around 1982 from Dane Bank College looking over the rooftops of Kingsway and Franklyn Avenue. In the foreground are the playing fields of Ruskin Road School. Many of Crewe's well-known landmarks are clearly visible from the vantage point, for instance, St Paul's Church, Hightown, St Mary's Roman Catholic Church, Delamere House, Big Bill Clock Tower, Christ Church and two of the many chimneys that adorned the Crewe horizon for many years. The two chimneys in the picture were at Flag Lane and Wistaston Road, and were both demolished nearly two decades ago.

Also evident in the view are the former Joiners Shop and the railway with the Company's General Offices in the background. After just over a hundred years since they were built, the railways moved offices and they became vacant. Various plans were put forward on how best to retain them but unfortunately before any firm decision had been made, the problem was resolved. The town's older generation will no doubt remember that on the evening of Saturday 23 July 1983, it was engulfed by fire and destroyed. The Joiners Shop, whose roof spanned between the two previous mentioned chimneys and was part of the railway's Deviation Works, was also later demolished. Nowadays a new road goes through much of this area serving a recent supermarket development.

The view also encapsulates a large part of land commonly known as the Walthall Vale. In the town's early history, the Walthalls owned quite a lot of land in the area. Reliable information says that the family were strongly opposed to any alcoholic drink and therefore insisted that no drinking establishment should ever be built within their estate. As all the pubs are situated on the periphery, this information seems to be correct.

. . . .

Many former residents believe that the Lyceum Theatre owes its existence to the larger pubs. Records show that in 1867 there were at least five pubs with Music Hall acts regularly appearing. These were: Oak Farm, the Adelphi, the Engine, the Vine Hotel and the Express. However, by 1878, that type of entertainment had ceased as the Lyceum took on the role of Music Hall. Before their demise all five hotels had been extensively

Adelphi Hotel, Market Street, c. 1962.

The Engine, Mill Street, c. 1929.

used for Vaudeville acts and ultimately resorted to a more local type of entertainment and a much wider range of pub pastimes.

A prominent advertisement in the local press of 1867 suggests that the Oak Farm was the more notable and possibly the most widely-used; the other four undoubtedly disputed that. All of them claimed that their entertainment was the best for christy minstrels, sentimental and comic singing, duets, dancing and other talents. They also all publicly announced that their wines, spirits and ales were of the finest quality with cheapest prices anywhere within the town.

Stiltons, Earle Street, c. 1981.

Cheese Hall Hotel, Earle Street, c. 1953.

Cheese Hall, Stiltons and finally The Three Lamps are the names this Hotel at 15 Earle Street has possessed during its 150 years of existence. Its first name was undoubtedly linked to the close proximity of the original Cheese Hall, now the Market Hall. John Hill, who built the Market Hall in 1854, had built it primarily for the sale of cheese. The Hall, supported by the sale of other dairy products, continued in its use until after the death of Hill in 1868. In 1869 it was unsurprisingly decided that it would be of more benefit to the locals as a general market. Consequently, when a Hotel was built on the opposite corner, 'Cheese Hall' had historic significance.

Whilst many older residents still refer to it as the Cheese Hall, the general populace believes that its present name is more appropriate, especially as it was named after a well-known Crewe landmark. The Three Lamps were originally on Hightown opposite the Jubilee Gardens. After being there for almost 100 years, they were moved to the Jubilee Gardens because of road alterations. Unfortunately the site was unsuitable and they were vandalised, being moved before they were totally destroyed. In a revamp of Earle Street in 1994, they were given pride of place on the corner of Earle Street and Market Street. Widespread agreement within the town suggests that Richard Whittle, who had originally given these lamps to the town when he was Mayor in 1880, would be delighted that his Three Lamps are still in use today, albeit at a different location.

. . . .

The Forrester's Arms, built around 1852, was converted by the Council into a suite of offices in 1893. Although the building was nothing spectacular and hopelessly overcrowded, it remained in use for the best part of ten years. The current Council building now stands on the site of this pub, which was demolished in 1902 shortly followed by a hairdresser's shop, a small disused chapel, and the Market Tavern, another pub.

The notices to quit did not please the hairdresser's shop or the pub. Mrs M. Higgins, the tenant of the Market Tavern, complained that she had spent considerable amounts of her own money in keeping the premises in a good state of repair therefore, when the time came for her to vacate, she hoped that the Council would suitably compensate her. In September 1902, the tenant of the hairdresser's gave up possession and the shop became empty. The Market Tavern became empty in early 1903, thus allowing the demolition of all the properties between the Market Hall and The Crown Hotel.

In May 1902, the Borough Surveyor advertised in the National Press for architects to submit plans and estimates for a new building, the first prize being £50. There were entries from over thirty architects, and eventually the winner was declared as Henry T. Hare. His trademark, a hare, appears in the corner of two of the windows on the main staircase. In November 1902 he was given instructions to proceed with the development of the building.

On 23 September 1903, the Mayor, James Henry Moore, laid the foundation stone. The builders were Robert Neill and Sons of Manchester, the contract price being £14,752, although the total cost, including furnishing fees and expenses, was in the region of £20,000. The 1905 Mayor, Arthur Griffiths Hill opened the new English Baroque-style Municipal Offices on 19 July 1905.

The front of the building is in Coxbench stone and the rear in red-facing bricks. Earle Street frontage is ninety-one feet long in Classic Renaissance design with twenty-seven feet high Ionic columns flanking the front entrance. The front elevation is completed by

Market Hall
(Market Tavern
and Forresters
Arms alongside)
c. 1882.

three pairs of large reclining figures carved in relief by F.E.E. Schenck and surmounts the three centre openings. The demolition of the pubs and businesses had allowed for the finest architectural building in Crewe to be constructed.

Some pubs have played more of a major part than others in the town's history. The Borough Arms, built in 1867, is for instance one of the last remaining beerhouses licensed before 1869. Before 1904, when Balfour's Licensing Act came into existence, Licensing Committees could refuse or grant a licence almost as they pleased, with the exception of those licensed before May 1869. Those built prior to 1869 could not be refused a license except on personal unsuitability of the applicant or because the premises were in a dirty or unclean condition.

The Borough Arms was built for and owned by James Atkinson, a railway doctor and the first Mayor of Crewe. He lived at Mirion House, which was about half a mile from this establishment. Rather than run it himself, he installed a tenant landlord. The pub is better known as Potters Bar – named this after a former landlord who was from the potteries.

Pubs have always arranged trips for their customers and the 1912 trip from the Borough Arms fitted in with that tradition. Before the First World War, these were men-only trips, although women appear pleased to have been photographed before it departed.

Curiously, many of the town's beerhouses appear in records long before they have a name. Although shown as a beerhouse for a number of years, it was 1892 before the Old Vaults at last appears with a name. Situated on the corner of Cobden and Earle Street, locals generally referred to it as the Pig and Whistle. The photograph taken about 1923 shows a local milk delivery from a horse-drawn float. Alongside the milk float are the Froggatt family who ran the pub for over twenty years. It was converted into a shop in late 1934, but may better remembered as one of its final uses, that of a second-hand jewellery and antique shop.

Municipal buildings, Earle Street, *c*. 1908.

The Old Vaults, Earle Street, c. 1922.

Shop on the corner of Cobden Street, c. 1964.

Borough Arms, Earle Street, c. 1912.

Blue Cap Dog and Grand Junction Hotels, Market Street, c. 1919.

This fascinating view of Market Street of the local people getting ready to celebrate the end of the First World War was taken in 1919. Peace could finally be celebrated! Decorations would adorn the town in a number of locations with this section of Market Street playing its part.

The ladder on the side of the Blue Cap indicates that the pub is getting ready for the ensuing celebrations. The Grand Junction and the Blue Cap Dog were suitably adorned, enabling them both to play their part. No doubt, it was a great relief after the end of a bloody and harrowing war.

The Blue Caps' most important role in history occurs during the late Victorian times. It concerned the way in which some of the larger breweries treated their tenants little better than paid skivvies. Furthermore, many of them were being evicted for the most trivial of cases often within a week. Obviously, this had an effect on the way that tenant landlords treated the pub and customers alike. Everyone became aware that something had to be done to change the situation.

In 1893, the local Licensing Committee took up the challenge and postponed the renewal of ten licences including all Walker's pubs of which the Blue Cap Dog was one. Unfortunately this was overturned at the next Quarter Sessions. Nevertheless, the fight to get better conditions for the tenants had begun. This stand by the Crewe Licensing Committee had reverberations throughout the whole of Britain, resulting in some minor improvements. The resolute attitude of the Crewe Bench inspired great numbers of magistrates throughout the country to examine the plight of their tenants.

Finally, after a long fight, the 1904 Licensing Act gave tenants of pubs of the larger breweries the same conditions as the 1869 beerhouses. This meant that each applicant was granted or refused a licence on its own merits. The licensees were delighted; no longer could the breweries dismiss them on a trivial pretext. The remarkable improvements that took place with the coming of these new conditions in the Crewe public houses eventually led to its adoption nationwide. The Crewe Agreement eventually became a quotation in law books on licensing.

After ninety-four years since its original construction, the Grand Junction needed redevelopment. It would provide better living accommodation and would see the height of the building change. It would no longer be single-storied, but in allowing for improvements, would become two. The lower photograph shows the work nearing completion in February 1938. This new and improved Grand Junction was officially opened on 14 April of that year.

Before the opening ceremony took place, the interior experienced radical changes with great emphasis being placed on the railway's influence within the town. The developers eventually tailored the lounge as a fitting tribute to the railwaymen of Crewe. Three model locomotives were proudly exhibited in this revamped lounge and they were the Rocket, the Lion and the recently-constructed streamlined Coronation. When it was finally finished, the lounge was lavishly fitted out in Indian Laurel with chromium fittings and luxurious maroon-leather seating.

Grand Junction Hotel, Victoria Street, c. 1936.

Swan Hotel and Grand Junction Hotel, Victoria Street, c. 1938.

Co-operative Street – Masonic
Arms at the far end, c. 1900.

The Masonic Arms,
Market Street, c. 1979.

Pubs have played more than a passing role in the evolution and growth of this Borough.
The first horse-drawn omnibus service started from the George in West Street in 1882.
In 1878, Fredrick Winby, a well-known local entrepreneur envisaged a three-foot
tramway from the Lion and Swan to the Royal Hotel. Significantly, in 1864 the original
Bessemer in Bessemer Street was demolished to enable the Company to build a steel-
making plant.

  The pub, in many people's eyes has always been the community's meeting place and the
  Masonic Arms was no different than the rest. When it first opened it was frequented by both
  locals and workers from the Co-op's substantial workforce. First licensed in 1868 as The
  Freemason Arms, it became the Masonic Arms eight years later. The top photograph shows the
  view from Whitegates towards the pub along past the Co-Op Bakery and Cabinet Maker

workshops. Unfortunately this was another town pub that suffered from the movement of local residents in the early 1970s. After being in decline for a number of years through the lack of customers, redevelopment of this area saw it demolished during 1983-84.

. . . .

The Nags Head in Market Street was the venue not only of the usual card and dominoes games but also had a boxing gymnasium in its upstairs rooms for a number of years. This particular enterprise encouraged young up-and-coming local boxers. In 1912, boxing booths situated behind the Market were frequented by locals trained at this pub. Mr

Above Nags Head, Market Street.

Right Lower End of Market Street, 1965.

Phillips, the landlord, even went a stage further. He was responsible for organizing some professional tournaments at the Lyceum Theatre, and of course featured some local amateurs trained at the Nags Head. Just before the First World War, the pub laid claim that it was producing some of the town's most promising boxers.

Over the years, the pub has seen not only locals and talented boxers but also quite a number of workers from the local foundry. Almost opposite the pub was a foundry built in 1878 for a firm trading under the name of Button and Brocklehurst. Later, an amalgamation saw it become the well-known Crewe firm of Carrington and Button. When built, its main entrance was in Water Street. However, ten years later, the street became Foundry Street. That name sufficed for a number of years until it became the bottom end of Meredith Street. Although the Button's foundry has been closed for many years, its legacy can still be readily seen on grid covers in and around the town.

. . . .

Many of the town's older residents would argue the Bull entry was a bigger boon to the town than the pub ever was. The pub was one of the original thirteen built for the impending influx of railway workers. Built in early spring of 1845, it fronted two major roads that would successfully serve the early townspeople of the area. With the arrival of the railways these two roads became Earle Street and Market Street. Both had a major impact on the Railway Company's settlement serving as early corridors linking the town together. The arrival of the worker's families saw both become main shopping streets and an ideal site for a pub.

This was another pub that in its early history had a blacksmith renting a yard at the rear. When first built, the archway into the yard had a large wooden gate affixed to it. Access to the yard could be gained through the gate or from Market Terrace. Although it was closed every Good Friday, early residents readily accepted this quick route from Market Terrace to Market Street. In its early history however, it was a dirty smelly cinder track that everyone in the Borough complained about. The problem was tackled in 1935 when it became a well-known cobbled and lighted alleyway. Regretfully in many resident's eyes, after decades of use the Bull entry was finally closed and, along with the pub, was demolished in late summer of 1961.

. . . .

When the Commercial Hotel was built in the spring of 1844, the main line to Chester went under Chester Bridge. Its close proximity to the Chester line led to some early inhabitants referring to it as the Station pub. Its unusual position on the slope of two inclines enabled it to have a bar stretching nearly eighteen yards down High Street. This unusual construction allowed customers a three-door access to it and right up to its demolition, the long-bar was well-used by local workmen.

Originally, its main customers were men from the Company's workforce. These men also worked in dreadful conditions and needed a simple form of relaxation. Early records reveal that although the workmen mostly used the bar, a different type of customer used the two-roomed lounge situated on the left of the main door. They were regularly used for cards and skittles by a number of well-known local businessmen.

Two local businessmen provide an amusing little tale from the early twentieth century. At the time, the shop next to the Commercial was a well-known jeweller named

Red Bull, Market Street, c. 1961.

New shops being built on the Red Bull site, c. 1962.

Commercial Hotel, Chester Bridge, c. 1961.

Wallworks. No more than thirty yards away on the corner of High Street opposite the pub was another jeweller named Moody. Two jewellers in such a short stretch of road must have been quite traumatic. They started to wait for the other to close, not daring to close too soon in case the other one picked up the trade. Eventually an errand boy from each firm was regularly sent to spy if the other business was showing any signs of closing. In due course, the lads wised up on how to finish early. They would meet discreetly in one of the Commercial's doorways agreeing to tell their bosses that the other one was about to close. They soon discovered that in this way, everyone was happy and all went home that much earlier.

In 1961, when the photograph was taken, Wallworks had long ceased trading and the Commercial was nearing closure. After Wallworks closed in 1933, the building had a number of ventures until late 1937 when it was converted into the Milk Bar, remaining as that use until its demolition. Although one jeweller had ceased trading, the other one was still quite active and being rebuilt in its changing surroundings. Bullocks, Woolridge and the Plaza cinema were all still being highly patronized, yet as is quite apparent, dramatic changes for this part of town were beginning to appear on the horizon.

four

South and East
of the Town

Duke of Bridgewater, Wistaston Road, c. 1952.

At this point, it might be helpful if an explanation was offered about the different types of drinking establishments that were available in Victorian Crewe. Three distinct types were clearly identifiable. They were the hotels and inns who can loosely be described as providing overnight accommodation for travellers, as well as serving to their alcoholic needs. It is also quite noticeable that in general the larger hotels were providing most of the function rooms during this period.

Next came the numerous beerhouses, their prime function being to sell beer. They provided lodgings only in special circumstances and very few offered any room facilities.

Both of these main alcoholic outlets were still supplemented further by a number of beer retailers and off-licences, who generally undercut the prices of the main outlets for their business.

A number of well-known pubs started their life as a normal dwellings but were then converted into beerhouses. These included: the Beech Tree Inn in Beech Street, the Duke of Bridgewater in Wistaston Road, the Rising Sun in Earle Street, Robin Hood in Nantwich Road, the Spread Eagle in Ludford Street, the Talbot Inn at 2 Stafford Street, the Stag in Wistaston Road, and the Lord Nelson in Mill Street. Over eighty per cent of these converted beerhouses were at some point extensively enlarged to cope with demand.

Built at the same time as Edleston Road bridge, the Duke of Bridgewater was originally nothing more than the converted front room of No. 2 Wistaston Road. It was perhaps named in rebellion, as the Duke was opposed to railways and their development – what better way to get even with the canal builder than by using his name for a pub in such close proximity to a main railway line? After being redeveloped on numerous occasions, it now sits snugly on the corner of Wistaston Road and Edleston Road but bears no resemblance to its initial beerhouse status.

Above Looking up Cross Street from the Beehive, c. 1934.

Right The Beehive, Oak Street, c. 1952.

In Dr W.H. Chaloner's book, *The Social and Economic Development of Crewe*, drink-related problems are explained in some detail. Towards the end of the nineteenth century, it became common knowledge that some residents, mostly men, were drinking to excess. This was often done at their families' expense and in most cases led to a breakdown of family life. Even in the face of this evidence, I still believe that during this period of history not enough was credited to the conditions that most workingmen had to endure. Obviously, relief of some description was required with alcohol becoming their easiest option.

In most instances, alcohol allowed escapism from their problems. The temperance movement in Crewe tried to eradicate the problem and between 1877 and 1896, no fresh full licenses were granted in the borough.

In 1881, the Borough contained forty-two hotels, forty-four beer-sellers and eight off-licenses. By 1892 those figures had reduced to forty-two, forty and seven respectively. This means that in an eleven-year period, four beerhouses and one off-license had closed. The four that closed and are lost forever in the antiquity of time were the Glove Inn in Herdman Street; the Beehive Inn in Oak Street; the Wellington Inn in Mill Street; and Island (Ireland) Green in Wistaston Road. In 1873, on the corner of Oak Street and Cross Street was the beerhouse, the Beehive. Although Cross Street itself has never had a beerhouse, Oak Street has had its fair share with the Beehive being just one of them. This pub was refused its license renewal in 1883 and ceased trading. After that, it became a lodging house, shop or a private dwelling for the remainder of its existence until it was finally demolished in 1952.

· ·

The High Street has always been the main thoroughfare through the area and onto the south of the town. During its early days, it was little more than a cart track. 1845 saw it being well-used by the town's inhabitants although the conditions of the street were described as quite deplorable. It was often knee-deep in clay and it was quite common for residents to lose their shoes in the deep mud. Slowly as the town expanded, the street improved and better road and pavement conditions came about. Some ten years later, not only was the Commercial well-established but the street had become a well-frequented shopping area. During this period, its pub capacity increased with the introduction of two well-known yesteryear pubs, the Dog and Partridge and the Old Vaults.

Around 100 years later, it was pretty clear that a total redevelopment of this street and the surrounding area was urgently required. At times, traffic conditions in the street were quite chaotic and road improvements were desperately needed. To assist the Council in their deliberations, Harry Bullock, a well-known photographer who was also a leading Councillor was commissioned by the Council to take photographic evidence. Bullock took the High Street photographic evidence on Friday 18 February 1938 at 12:10pm with the ensuing photograph being officially signed by him.

Although very few locals at the time were aware, evidence for redevelopment for this and many areas of the town was being gathered. The drivers who were slowly negotiating the street were at least able to see that the Commercial was about to have a fresh coat of paint. The Old Vaults, rebuilt in 1932, was now called Kettells and had become a leading entertainment centre. The one sad note from 1938 in the area's drinking establishments is that the Royal Oak Hotel, just visible through the mist, was no longer in use.

Preceding page High Street, c. 1938.

· ·

In the town's early history, the first pub anyone encountered on leaving via Mill Street would have been the Royal Oak Hotel. Built in late 1846, it was situated on the corner where High Street and Mill Street combine. Up to 1936, when it finally closed, hundreds of residents would pass this pub each week and use the iron-bridge short cut. No doubt some in the crowd had crossed the bridge to see the 1906 Hospital Fête procession pass the pub on its way to Crewe Hall, its venue for that year. After closure, it lay derelict for over ten years, but that didn't prevent it from being directly hit by an incendiary bomb in 1941.

Right The Royal
Oak, Mill Street,
c. 1906.

Below Neptune
Inn, Mill Street.
c. 1913.

Diagonally opposite the Royal Oak was the Neptune which supplemented its trade by appealing to residents using the Company's baths, built next to the Royal Oak in 1866. Apparently, for a number of years it was quite successful in attracting customers who, on leaving the baths, would call for a pint whilst relaxing with a game of cards, dominoes or perhaps even the gentleman's game of billiards.

The Company's bath facility was appreciated by almost everyone. It consisted of plunge and slipper baths, supported by a Turkish bath. The pool itself was a simple fill and empty type. It had no heating, filtration or circulation systems, the water was just changed on a weekly basis. To compensate for this, admission charges were reduced as the week continued. Nevertheless, they were in constant use for just over seventy years. The Neptune, the Royal Oak and the baths, having been empty since just before the Second World War, were demolished during early 1950.

George and Dragon, Mill Street, c. 1899.

A pub long-forgotten located on the corner of Mill and Brook Streets was the George and Dragon. This pub had a rather short existence, being converted from a large house during 1861, but ceasing trade in 1909. It provided the usual types of leisure pursuits for the local inhabitants but from 1867 gained more trade through the building of the Enginemen's Barracks, just opposite it. These Barracks, built to accommodate engine drivers and firemen who found it necessary for an overnight stay, were in a prime location to offer their lodgers a pint from across the road.

On closing, it was acquired by F. Whiston & Co. pressed metal picture frame and umbrella manufacturers, and makers of metal furniture and a type of pram. Surprisingly, not only were the goods sold widely in this country but also it had quite a significant export business. Its success is illustrated by its employment of over 120 women and girls in the height of its production. After the First World War, production increased at such a rapid pace that it was decided to demolish the old pub along with its adjoining property, allowing the firm to build a brand new factory.

The photograph was taken on 16 October 1899 and shows the Second Cheshire Royal Engineers (Railway Volunteers) marching under Mill Street Bridge past the pub on their way to serve in the Boer War. This army was formed and introduced by Francis W. Webb in 1887. It consisted purely of volunteers all of whom were employed by the Company. They proved to be particularly successful during the Boer War campaign in driving armoured trains, building and repairing bridges, as well as working on all kinds of heavy track-laying machinery. After becoming part of the Territorial Army in 1908 and with continuing dwindling support, they were disbanded in March 1912.

Above The Imperial Hotel, Edleston Road, c. 1963.

Right Imperial Hotel date stone, Chapel Street, c. 1979.

In 1876, any Edleston Road development was still in its infancy, however; buildings would soon begin to appear. During that year, on the corner of Chapel Street and Edleston Road, the new Police Station was built. This replaced the early one that had been constructed in Wistaston Street (Eaton Street). As time progressed, it had become too small to deal with the growing population and the consequent increase in crime. It became imperative that it be replaced.

Just over two years later, the opposite corner of Edleston Road would witness the building of the Imperial Hotel. Its first landlord would be John Badger, who was succeeded by his son Alfred. Alfred successfully served on Crewe's Council for many years until becoming Mayor for 1927. This was quite a historic year in the annals of Crewe history. It was the year that saw the celebration for the Jubilee of Crewe with the opening of the Jubilee Gardens. Alfred Badger and Sir William Hodgson, a local doctor who resided at Helmsville, laid the foundation stones for the gardens. On the same day both were granted the freedom of the Borough for their service to the townspeople of Crewe.

The continuing changing face of a street is adequately illustrated by Mill Street, which was originally named Mill Lane due to the mill by the river being used by monks from Combermere Abbey. After the railways arrived, the building of churches, shops, houses and pubs would witness its first transformation. However, in 1850, seven years since the first workers had been transferred here from Edge Hill, it was already a different picture. A Victorian writer vividly gives an account of a visit to the station and this area:

> On arrival at the station, the only way of entrance and exit was through a close-shut iron gate. Beside the gate stood a policeman looking with enviable coolness at all the bustle that was going on around him. 'Where is Crewe?' I said to the guardian of the iron gate. 'Cross the bridge, go straight on and turn to the right', was the reply.
>
> So I crossed the bridge and found myself in a pleasant country road [Nantwich Road]. The flat fields of Cheshire extended on the right [looking towards the town centre] and to the left [looking towards Gresty]. In the distance, about half a mile away, appeared the square massive tower of a church [Christ Church] surrounded by long ranges of low buildings like workshops [the Company's works – Forge etc.]. Seemingly attached to the tower were rows of buildings evidently quite new [the shops and houses around the new settlement]. Some neat cottages lined the sides of the road and there were two or three inns [Royal Hotel and possibly Egerton Arms] all bearing the signs of youth.
>
> Turning to the right [Mill Lane], I passed a Methodist Chapel bearing the date of its erection of 1848 [corner of Mill Lane/Chapel Street], a new flourmill driven by water [the site of the original mill], a new inn with a brave new signboard [perhaps the Royal Oak], and crossing the boundary made by the Chester line [the original line to Chester by the works], I arrived in Crewe.

That was how this traveller saw Crewe Station and its surrounding area – as little more than a rural settlement.

In fifty years, the railway's influence dramatically changed the rural nature of Crewe. The view down Mill Street in 1900 from the Engine Hotel is self-explanatory and shows how it had become one of the town's main commercial streets. During this period, successful businesses were flourishing within the town and Mill Street was no exception. The street also thrived with the usual pub entertainment provided by no less than eleven outlets: starting at the Albion Inn, then the Express Hotel, Lord Nelson, the Engine

Mill Street, looking towards the town centre, c. 1900.

Hotel and the Anchor Inn. On the other side of the road was the Globe Inn, the George and Dragon, the Rams Head and the Neptune Inn. Right in the corner of Mill Street and High Street was the last pub, the Royal Oak Hotel.

· ·

In 1868, the Cannon Inn at 1 Bank Street was probably one of the smallest beerhouses within the town's boundaries. Early reminiscences seem to suggest that its name, along with that of the Lord Nelson and the Wellington Arms, were in memory of the Battle of Trafalgar.

The landlady, Ann Evans, sold beer to support her family. These times, long before the emergence of the Welfare State and benefits, were especially hard times for the working classes, and so people had to work hard to stave off malnutrition, hunger and disease.

The Cannon Inn was in a cul-de-sac off Lockitt Street with twenty-five terraced houses. It backed on to the North Sheds. Lockitt Street was also home to the town's first gasworks. During its existence, this street has had at least three unnamed beerhouses. Along with the Cannon, this gave the area four drinking establishments, providing a meeting place for the locals as well as somewhere they could relax with their workmates and colleagues.

Site of the Cannon Inn, Bank Street, c. 1957.

View from Bank Street looking down Lockitt Street, c. 1964.

The pubs' involvement was again apparent during April 1913 when King George V and Queen Mary were to honour the town with a highly successful two-day visit during that year. Most of the town took part and it was extensively decorated for what was regarded as probably one of Crewe's most important days. Nearly every public and private building was adorned with decorations. The Engine played its part in the ensuing celebrations. Locals tell me that not only were they most pleased with the pub's effort but even more so with the penny-off-a-pint price at which beer was sold all week.

The Engine Hotel, Mill Street, *c.* 1913

Mill Street looking towards the Engine, *c.* 1954.

The view from the Express towards Union Street in 1954 shows the abundance of shops on the east side of Mill Street. Once one of the main shopping areas of the town, the thoughts of redevelopment at this time were high on the agenda. The demolition of the east side of the street from the Express to the bridge was eventually in full swing by 1968, although it was not until 1969 that two more of the town's pubs were obliterated forever, those being the Lord Nelson and the Engine Hotel.

Two former pubs in Station Street were the Queens Hotel and the Railway Inn. Along with the Sterling Tap, they primarily dealt with the men from the sheds. The North Steam Sheds, at the end of Station Street, had many thousands of railway men through its archway during its lifetime, offering jobs with extremely demanding and dirty conditions. No doubt at the end of the shift relief, solace was sought in these three pubs. Tales abound about men during the nineteenth and twentieth centuries waiting in the Queens to be called for work. Nowadays this may seem strange, but in the days of 'employment as required', it was possibly the only way for men urgently seeking work to find employment.

Over the years, the Queens Hotel, photographed with its last landlord, Dan Riley Jnr, acquired the nickname the Big Cabin because of its close proximity to the sheds – only a nine-inch wall separated the two.

Dan Riley became the landlord in 1948, taking over from his father who had been there since 1932. There was a certain amount of controversy when he did succeed his father due to his young age. He was twenty-three at the time and had served in the forces, but the Magistrates nevertheless felt he was not old enough to run a pub. However, he proved them wrong and successfully ran the pub from 1948 until its closure in 1969.

Left Queens Hotel, Station Street, c. 1968.

Below Railway Inn, Station Street, c. 1968.

The Railway Inn shown on the previous page with its last landlady Mrs Ellis was another favourite with the locals after a rigorous day of work. The pub, its door directly on the corner of Wesley Street and Station Street served the needs of both locals and men from the 'sheds' for decades.

In 1968, the Council's continuing slum clearance policy meant that fifty-eight shops and houses in Station Street, including the Railway Hotel and the Sterling Tap, were demolished. Left standing in isolation for a while was the Queens Hotel, although that was demolished along with the two Mill Street pubs (the Lord Nelson and the Engine) in 1969.

The Brunswick Hotel, Nantwich Road, c. 1922.

The Robin Hood, Nantwich Road, c. 1925.

It is well-documented that the Steam Engine in Mill Street hosted the twenty-seventh AGM of the Crewe and Coppenhall Association for the protection of Felons in 1869, but is not so widely known that many of the other pubs allowed their premises to be used for formal meetings. For instance, the Amalgamated Society of Railway Servants met regularly at the Brunswick Hotel on Nantwich Road. Opposite the Brunswick is a display hoarding advertising HP sauce. This was the entrance to a cul-de-sac street of twelve houses sandwiched between Chambers Street and South Street named Fareham's Row.

Not only were pubs used for those meetings, but they were also widely used for various leisure pursuits. Both the Brunswick Hotel and the Robin Hood were no strangers to the normal pub games. Both were well frequented by the darts and dominoes players, whilst years ago, the Robin Hood was packed when skittles matches were being played. This pub, one of the original eight beerhouses was situated about fifty yards nearer to Mill Street. It finally closed its doors in 1937. After a number of other uses, it was demolished and the site was totally redeveloped in around 1961.

· ·

This 1923 view from Ruskin Road shows just how well the Earl of Crewe blended in with its surrounding environment. Built in 1897 reputedly on the site of a former eighteenth-century beerhouse, its construction coincided with the Diamond Jubilee of Queen Victoria, the year being splendidly captured in a commemorative stone in the apex of the main roof. The stone itself is a terracotta panel depicting Queen Victoria, surrounded by names of the leading countries of the British Empire. The gesture by the builder shows how well her sixty-year celebrations were received.

Although the pub is named after the Lord of the Manor, that could never have been envisaged with his early contacts with the town. The third Baron, who became the Right Honourable Lord Crewe, made no bones about how he despised the railways and their

Earl of Crewe, Nantwich Rd, c. 1922.

Terracotta Panel, c. 1980.

ruination of his land. He also ordered his workmen to plant trees along Weston Road to blot out their impact and told his coachman never to drive him past the station but to take alternative routes to get to other parts of the area.

Over the years, Lord Crewe mellowed in his thoughts about the railways and long before his death in 1894 he had become a friend of a number of high-ranking railway officials. His friendship with Sir Richard Moon and Francis Webb ensured he was the guest of honour at most railway functions. He was their guest of honour at both the Queens Golden Jubilee celebration and Queens Park dedication in 1887 as well as the official opening of Queens Park on 9 June 1888.

Nowadays, modern society passes without even a cursory glance and who could blame them. The pub has sacrificed much of its charm through over-modernisation. Furthermore, to the disappointment of many residents, even its name has changed to just The Earl. Residents from far and wide believe that was a retrograde step and that its original name should be reinstated, especially when they realise it was named in tribute to the family whose ancestral home gave its name to the town.

⋅ ⋅

On Tuesday morning, 4 July 1837, when the first passenger train stopped at a sleepy little halt called Monks Coppenhall, I imagine that very few people realised what a tremendous impact it would have on the area. A dairy produce fair had been set up just outside the station on the Nantwich–Wheelock turnpike road. The area around the Halt thronged with excited people from the surrounding districts, not only wanting to visit the fair, but to have their first look at this new Iron Horse.

At 8.45 a.m. that morning, with black smoke belching from its tall chimney, the local people had their first glimpse of the train as it slowly pulled into Monks Coppenhall. This first inaugural journey was hauled by a steam locomotive numbered forty-nine and named *Dr. Dalton*. It stopped for about eleven minutes at the station and after refuelling and taking on water, continued on its history-making journey to Birmingham. The driver of the train, James Middleton, would have his own piece of Crewe history for fifty years. Later he would unveil the clock in Queens Park.

Less than three years after that momentous occasion, this area witnessed the building of the Royal Hotel. The site was to be roughly the same spot where the fair had been held. During this period, expansion was very rapid because in 1841 the hotel became the

The Royal Hotel, Nantwich Rd, c. 1907.

town's first post office. Prior to this, a man had gone to Nantwich three times a week to collect the mail, and a number of houses in Manchester and Forge Street received it. Although at first, the hotel was still only a receiving house, the local population soon discovered there was a vast improvement. In March 1846, the Royal Hotel had its status lifted up from a receiving house to Sub-Post Office of Nantwich. Then a few weeks later, in July 1846, it was further enhanced and became a Post Office in its own right. From these humble beginnings one of the country's biggest distribution centres for the Royal Mail would arise over the years.

Extensively-rebuilt during late-Victorian times, one of the most interesting views of the Hotel was on the approach from the Sandbach direction. Clearly visible in different coloured roof slates were the words Royal Hotel, Billiards and Posting. The word 'posting' has nothing to do with postal services previously mentioned but its stabling facilities. Obviously, over the years, the Hotel has seen many renovations. Regretfully, the latest renovation has seen the wording 'Legend' in the slates being covered by a coat of paint; another piece of the town's history was lost.

In 1892, the main Breweries in the town were Sir A.B. Walker (Liverpool) with nearly a dozen pubs selling their beer; Greenhall Whitley (Warrington) again with nearly a dozen pubs under their wing; North Cheshire Brewery Limited had seven pubs whilst Crewe's own Brewery (South Cheshire – Woolfs) had six. Even the Railway Company (LNWR) had three, whilst Charles Welch owned two, his main pub being the Royal Hotel in Nantwich Road whilst his other one was the Robin Hood, again in Nantwich Road. Private breweries supplied a further eight and finally Boddingtons and Wilsons had just

Crewe Arms Hotel, Nantwich Rd, c. 1904.

over a dozen between them. That was how the alcohol was distributed to the seventy-four pubs of Crewe during in this period.

Wrapped up in the town's history, quite a number of pubs have left their mark, some demolished many years ago whilst others still provide a leisure outlet. Although not common knowledge, but Queen Victoria stayed at the original Crewe Arms on 30 September 1849. She was on her way from Balmoral back to the capital. The journey in those days was exceptionally long so it was felt that an overnight stay at the Crewe Arms Hotel would be an ideal resting place. The landlord, Mr William Edwards, with a candle lit candelabra, met her at the station. He escorted the Queen and her entourage through a back entrance to ensure her privacy was maintained. Rumours abounded, saying that her own linen was seen being taken from the train and into the Hotel. Privately questions were asked in the town, 'was the hotel's linen seemingly not good enough?'

The current Crewe Arms was built in 1880 as the date on the roof boldly proclaims. Following the same pattern in other railway towns, this is another good example of a railway-built hotel. Victorian England was all about railways, the ever-increasing railway-travelling public and their demands being catered for. When it was built, horses also had to be attended to, for they had a major role to play in the local transport. The gentleman is standing by the archway that led into a cobbled yard with stables at the rear. Further along the front can be seen the workshop where carriages were made ready.

Even nowadays, both the exterior and interior of the hotel are worth a close examination. Above both the main doorway and just in front of the chimneys is the Crewe family coat of arms. The interior is of classic design with marble fireplaces that give it the warm, rich quality that most railway hotels seemed to possess. When built, it was done to the highest possible quality and design. That quality can still be appreciated because of the way it has successfully weathered the passage of time.

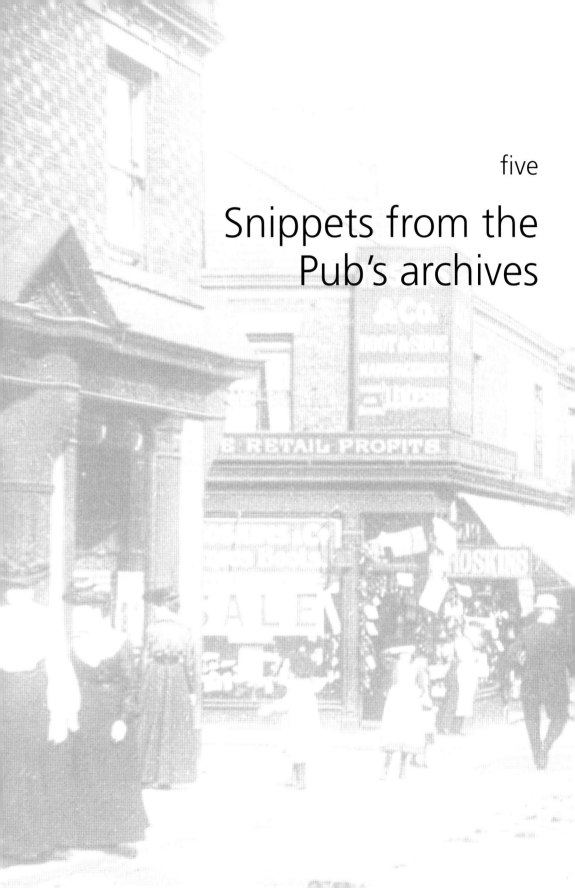

five

Snippets from the Pub's archives

September 1874

A thousand miles in a thousand hours – Madame Wilett still continues to perform her arduous task of trying to complete a thousand miles in a thousand hours at the Sydney Arms Recreation Ground. The lady will have completed over half her task on Saturday 17 when, in the afternoon, she will parade through the principal streets of Crewe accompanied by a brass band.

September 1877

The marriage took place on Wednesday 19 of Councillor Charles Welch, Royal Hotel, Nantwich Road and Miss Furber of The Castle Hotel, Heath Street. A reception for 100 guests was held at the Royal Hotel. Mr Wilding, the well-known confectioner of Linden Grange, supplied a 60lb wedding cake with a height of 4ft.

January 1878

Before Crewe Magistrates was Thomas Bradburn, Inn Keeper of the Talbot Inn, West Street, charged with allowing his premises to be used for gambling. He was accused of permitting customers the playing of dominoes for beer and cigars. After the evidence had been heard, the Bench were divided on his guilt, therefore the case was dismissed.

March 1878

On Wednesday 27 March at 10 p.m. neighbours were alarmed to see fire and smoke bellowing from one of the Longford cottages by the side of the Brunswick Hotel. Mr Sibley, the Manager of Rylands Works opposite, sent for the volunteer Fire Brigade. However, before they arrived he organized for the fire to be tackled by the use of fire buckets. He was later praised for his public duty in containing the fire.

June 1878

Chester Northgate and Lion Breweries are selling in their Crewe pubs. Ale at one shilling a gallon. It is for sale in four-and-a-half, nine, eighteen or thirty-six-gallon casks.

July 1899

Plans were submitted and eventually approved for a new Hotel on the corner of Hungerford Avenue and Hugerford Road. The approval was given subject to the frontage line in Hungerford Road being maintained and not protruding in the north west direction.

. . . .

April and July 1909

Plans were submitted and approved for the conversions of two former Inns. The first was in April when permission was given to convert the New Inn, 106 Earle Street, into two retail shops. In July, the second permission was given to change the Talbot Inn, 2 Stafford Street, into two cottages.

. . . .

April 1912

An application was submitted and approved on behalf of Chester's Brewery for conversion of the former public house called the Laburnum Inn, 33 Thomas Street, into two cottages.

. . . .

September 1909

The Town Clerk read a letter from Mr R.W. Wadsley, Proprietor of the Castle Hotel, stating he would be obliged if the Committee could see their way clear to having the boxes removed from under the shed on the ground behind the Market, as they were the resting place for the loafers of the town. The noise and language around there on Sundays and other days was almost unbearable.

. . . .

November 1915

Approval was given for the conversion of the former Vernon Arms, Stafford Street, into two cottages for Councillor F.W. Withoff.

. . . .

August 1919

The Town Clerk read a letter to the Mayor dated the 18, from Mr Jas. H. Ravenscroft with reference to a proposal to construct a Light Railway. This Railway would be from the corner of Bridle Road and Wistaston Road, opposite to Hop Pole Hotel to the triangle at the Cottage Hospital by Queens Park. The Town Clerk was instructed by the Committee to obtain costs of providing the necessary power to ensure this Light Railway system could be implemented.

. . . .

June 1929

The water-wheel of the former Woolf's brewery on the river in the Valley Park was in need of repair, reported the Town Clerk. He informed the committee that Mr Brockleshurst of Ind Coope had seen him on several occasions with reference to the Corporation putting the wheel back in working order. Mr Button had been approached and had submitted a quotation of £7.17s 6d. It was recommended that the Council accepts that bid.

. . . .

November 1933

At the General Purposes Committee meeting, the Town Clerk read a letter from Messrs Robert Bygott & Sons enquiring whether the Corporation would be interested in the purchase of the empty premises formally known as The Rams Head at 174 Mill Street Crewe, which they had for disposal.

December 1935

The following Plan was submitted to the Council:

Proposed New Hotel, junction of Barker Street & Neville Street for Trelfalls Brewery Co.

Granted: Subject to the drainage and steelwork being to the satisfaction of the Borough Surveyor.

March 1937

Demolition took place of the Rams Head, 174 Mill Street, that had been empty for a number of years and was therefore in a derelict condition. The site on the corner of Oak Street and Mill Street was temporally fenced off awaiting new redevelopment.

August 1949

This was the year that saw the beginning of the demolition of properties in the Oak Street area. Not only would this demolition include the streets of Blackberry, Cross and Bowling Green but also the Royal Oak and Neptune pubs. Both had been empty since 1937 when both licences were surrendered in favour of a new pub – Ash Bank Hotel. The Royal Oak, when it was finally demolished in July 1950, was little more than a shell. This was because of bomb damage it had suffered by a high explosive bomb during the early part of the Second World War.

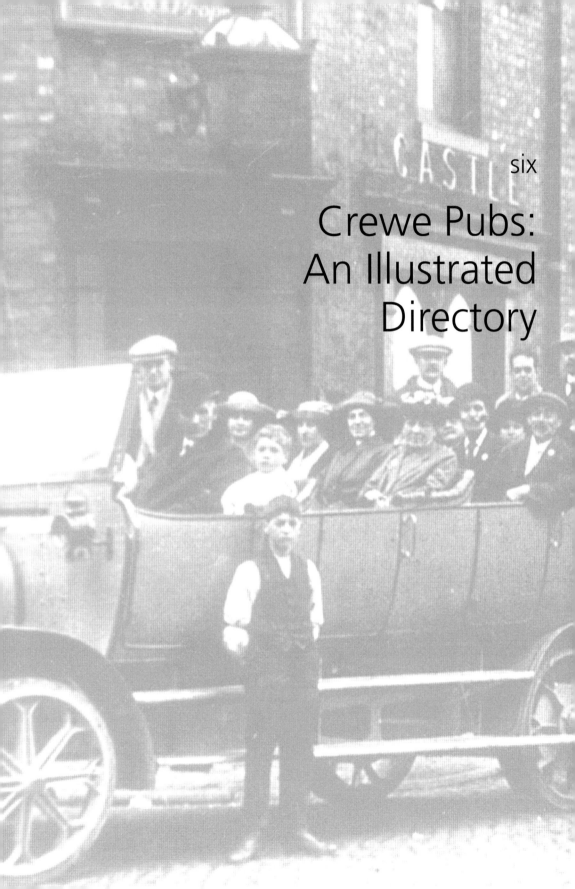

six

Crewe Pubs:
An Illustrated
Directory

Research carried out over many years has enabled the production of a fully comprehensive list of any 'pub' that has ever existed within Crewe. I believed it was important to create this list because, along with their addresses, it will finally dispel any lingering doubts as to where any pub was actually situated. I felt that such a record was needed to help in establishing a database for any future reference. To further help the reader, pubs which have been demolished or redeveloped are shown in *italics*.

Albion Inn, Mill Street, c. 1965.

Blue Cap Dog, Market Street, c. 1962.

Adelphi Hotel, 60 Market Street.
Albert Hotel, 64 Oakley Street.
Albion Inn, 23 Mill Street.
Anchor Inn, 159 Mill Street.
Angel Hotel, 25 Victoria Street.
Ashbank Hotel, 2 Pyms Lane.

. . . .

Beech Tree Inn, 55 Beech Street.
Beehive Inn, 11 Oak Street.
Bellevue Inn, 85 Earle Street.
Bessemer Hotel, 81 Peel Street.
Blackhorse Inn, Sandy Lane.
Blue Cap Dog, 68 Market Street.
Blue Bell Inn, Ford Lane.
Borough Arms, 33 Earle Street.
Bridge Inn, 91 Broad Street.
Bridge Tavern, Small Lane (now Earle
    Street).
British Lion Inn, 58 Nantwich Road.
Brunel Arms, 156 West Street.
Brunswick Hotel, 71 Nantwich Road.
Bulls Head Hotel, 124 West Street.
Burton Hotel, 81 Victoria Street.

. . . .

Cannon Inn, 1 Bank Street.
Captain Webb, 255 Underwood Lane.
Castle Hotel, 11 Heath Street.

Brunel Arms, West Street, *c.* 1989.

Castle Hotel, Heath Street, *c.* 1922.

Cheese Hall Hotel (The Three Lamps),
    15 Earle Street.
Chetwode Arms, 2 Albert Street.
Comfortable Jill, 17 Thomas Street.
Commercial Hotel, 3 Chester Bridge.
Crewe Arms Hotel, Nantwich Road.
Cross Keys Hotel, 2 Remer Street.
Crown Hotel, 25 Earle Street.
Cumberland Arms, 5 Middlewich
    Street.

Chetwode Arms, Albert Street, *c.* 1957.

. . . .

Delamere Arms (The Blazer), 1 Broom
    Street.
Dog and Partridge, 21 High Street.
Duke of Bridgewater, 2 Wistaston Road.

. . . .

Earl of Chester, 102/4 Wistaston Road.
Earl of Crewe, 198 Nantwich.Road.
Engine Hotel, 77 Mill Street.
Egerton Arms (The Barrel), 38 Nantwich
    Road.
Express Hotel, 39 Mill Street.

Earl of Crewe, Nantwich Road, *c.* 1907.

. . . .

Flying Lady, Coleridge Way.
Foresters Arms, 23 Earle Street.

. . . .

George Hotel, 645 West Street.
George & Dragon, 172 Mill Street.
Globe Inn, 168 Mill Street.
Golden Lion, 7 Oak Street.
Glove Inn, 17 Herdman Street.

Express Hotel, Mill Street, *c.* 1930.

George Hotel, West Street, c. 1908.

Grand Junction Hotel (now Heath Street),
   1 Victoria Street.

Harp Inn, 13 Stafford Street.
Horse Shoe Hotel, North Street.
Hope Pole Inn, 142 Wistaston Road.

Imperial Hotel, 183/5 Edleston Road.
Ireland Green, 91 Wistaston Road.

Kings Arms Hotel, 56/8 Earle Street.

Laburnum Inn, 33 Thomas Street.
Lamb Inn, 17 Oak Street.
Lion and Swan Hotel, 215 West Street.
Lord Nelson Inn, 61a Mill Street.
Lord Raglan, 95 Thomas Street.

Market Tavern, 17 Earle Street.
Masonic Arms, 94 Market Street.

Nags Head, 157 Market Street.
Neptune Inn, 188 Mill Street.
New Inn, 106 Earle Street.
North Western Hotel (became the
   Queens Hotel), 57 Station Street.

Oak Farm Hotel, 27 Oak Street.

Grand Junction, Victoria Street, c. 1979.

Lord Nelson,
Mill Street,
c. 1955.

Masonic Arms, Market Street, c. 1982.

Old Crown, Earle Street, c. 1913.

Old Crown, 67 Earle Street.
Old Vaults (Kettells), 25 High Street.
Old Vaults (Pig & Whistle), 31 Earle Street.
Old Vine Inn (closed 2003), 45 Flag Lane.

. . . .

Parkers Vaults, 129 Wistaston Road.
Prince of Wales Hotel, 120 West Street.

. . . .

Red Bull Hotel, Market Street, c. 1960.

Queens Hotel (formerly North Western
    Hotel), 57 Station Street.
Queens Park Hotel, 42 Wistaston Road.

. . . .

Railway Inn, 18 Station Street.
Rams Head, 174 Mill Street.
Raven Inn (rebuilt Brookhouse Drive),
    25 Dewes Street.
Red Bull Hotel, 53 Market Street.
Rifleman Hotel, 78 Beech Street.
Rising Sun, 130 Earle Street.
Robin Hood, 55 Nantwich Road.
Rockwood Hotel, 204 Alton Street.
Royal Hotel, 5/7 Nantwich Road.
Royal Oak Hotel, 191 Mill Street.
Royal Scot, Plane Tree Drive.

Rockwood Hotel, Alton Street, c. 1979.

. . . .

Spread Eagle, 7 Ludford Street.
Spring Tavern, 41 Broad Street.
Staffordshire Knot, 54 Victoria Street.
Stag Inn, 84 Wistaston Road.
Star Inn, 65 Victoria Street.
Sterling Tap, 4 Station Street.
Swan Hotel, 13 Victoria Street.

Royal Hotel, Nantwich Road, c. 1923.

. . . .

Talbot Inn, 2 Stafford Street.
The Globe, 24 Railway Street.
The Old Manor, Nantwich Road.

. . . .

Vernon Arms, 31 Stafford Street.
Victoria Hotel, 93 Victoria Street.
Vine Hotel, 41/43 Earle Street.

. . . .

Star Inn, Victoria Street, c. 1907.

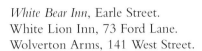

Victoria Hotel, Victoria Street, c. 1974.

View form the Old Vine Inn, Flag Lane, c. 1969.

White Bear Inn, Earle Street.
White Lion Inn, 73 Ford Lane.
Wolverton Arms, 141 West Street.

· ·

As well as the 100 or so pubs that have been mentioned, others remain firmly hidden in the depths of time. No matter how thoroughly records are searched to establish their authenticity, some are just impossible to verify. The only guidance to

their very existence is some vague references to them in an early newspaper. Nevertheless, they should be included in order to keep the record of pub names complete.

Game Cock Inn, Oak Street.
Golden Lion, Oak Street.
Jubilee Tavern, High Street.
Plasterers Arms, Thomas Street.
Wellington Arms, Mill Street.
White Bear Inn, Lawton Street

· ·

The photograph taken in the early 1970s shows a bustling Victoria Street thronged with shoppers. The Trustees Bank who had relocated from further up Victoria Street had acquired the site of the recently demolished Swan Hotel (Big Duck). Some major alterations had recently taken place in this street but over the next couple of decades many more were to follow. Fine Fare, who no longer have any presence in the town, had built a new store occupying the site of the former high-class confectioners of Wildings. On the right of the photograph is the Grand Junction Hotel. Eventually, this would also be demolished. The Angel is still clearly visible on the corner of Oakley Street but that too was soon to vanish from the skyline.

Victoria Street looking towards Hightown, *c.* 1972.

Other Cheshire titles published by Tempus include

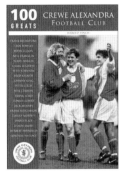

Crewe
BRIAN EDGE

Known as the town where people only went to change trains, readers will find their memories refreshed and enlightened by this evocative portrait of Crewe and the surrounding district. This selection of archive photographs and postcards captures the nostalgia of the years between 1895 and 1960 and illustrates the changing face of the town during this time, including the impact of the railway interchange.
0 7524 3004 1

Crewe Alexandra Football Club 100 Greats
HAROLD FINCH

Crewe Alexandra Football Club was formed in 1877 and went on to become founder members of the Football League Second Division in 1892. Long-serving members are included in this volume, but there are others whose time at the club may have been much shorter, but whose individual contributions are still talked about on a regular basis. Without these 100 players we would not have a club history or the wealth of memories that they bring to mind.
0 7524 3088 2

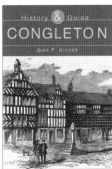

Cheshire Salt Country Then & Now
J. BRIAN CURZON

Winsford, Northwich and Middlewich have witnessed many changes over the last century. Compiled with over eighty pairs of images this volume captures life in these towns and surrounding villages as they once were, and compares them with how they look now. Vistas include the cotton mills and smoking chimneys of the salt industry, the horse-drawn coach on its way to Northwich market and salt barges on the River Weaver.
0 7524 2675 3

Congleton History & Guide
JOAN P. ALCOCK

This study, illustrated with over 100 photographs and archive ephemera, presents a chronological history of this Cheshire market town from Neolithic times to the twenty-first century. As well as recording local developments it also examines how events like the Plague, the Civil War and two world wars affected the town and contribute to its story. A feature of this book is a pair of walking tours which allow the reader to explore Congleton's history through its existing streets and buildings.
0 7524 2946 9

If you are interested in purchasing other books published by Tempus, or in case you have difficulty finding any Tempus books in your local bookshop, you can also place orders directly through our website

www.tempus-publishing.com